Recovery Church
His Story

How our stories became God stories.
How thousands of men and women
found faith and recovery.

Recovery Church Movement
Jupiter, FL

ISBN: 979-8-9868064-0-2

WWW.RECOVERY.CHURCH

Recovery Church Movement
10152 Indiantown Rd. #193
Jupiter, FL 33478
(561) 972-4142
Info@Recovery.Church
www.Recovery.Church

Author:	Recovery Church Movement Trust
Foreword:	T Freeman
Editor:	Rachel Hirsch
Compiled:	Philip Dvorak
Contributions:	RC family members
Formatting:	Philip Dvorak, Sara Dvorak & Michael Fashoda

ISBN: 979-8-9868064-0-2

ENDORSEMENTS

I've seen the Recovery Church movement in action. It's incredibly refreshing. Anyone who needs a beautiful vision of what 'church' really means; anyone who needs a renewed appreciation for the radical grace of God; anyone wanting to be reminded of the difference Jesus makes--this book, and these stories, are for you.

- Brant Hansen. Bestselling author and nationally syndicated radio host.

The Recovery Church story is remarkable. It is the story of Almighty God's redemptive, transformational power. It is the story of a mighty movement of God. It has been my great privilege to watch the RC story unfold from its early days. What God has done - and is doing - is nothing short of miraculous! As you read this story of stories, you will be reminded of and encouraged by what God can do with those willing to deny themselves, take up their crosses, and follow Him. Get ready to be blessed as you read what God has done!

- Dr. David Nelms. Founder & President of The Timothy Initiative.

Our society, families, and the Church are in mental health, addiction, and recovery disaster. Drug overdose is closely becoming one of the leading causes of death in the United States. A record 107,622 people in the U.S. died from overdoses in 2021. Think about that. We are in a desperate situation and the Church must take action. Recovery Church Movement is boldly taking that action. They are uniquely positioned as a bridge which allows people to find faith and a pathway to recovery. I highly recommend you read the story of how God, through Recovery Church, is using those who have recovered from substance use disorders to be the hands and feet of Jesus, helping others find hope and healing. I recommend every church leader wanting to provide an opportunity for those struggling with addictions to strongly consider partnering with Recovery Church Movement to start a Recovery Church in your community today.

- Dr. Tim Clinton. President of the American Association of Christian Counselors (AACC). *Co-Host of "Dr. James Dobson's Family Talk." Executive Director of the Global Center on Mental Health, Addiction and Recovery at Liberty University.*

The crisis of addiction is arguably the most critical problem facing the Church today. The Church needs to be asking, "How can we better respond?" Recovery Church is a great part of the answer. Recovery Church Movement helps bridge the gap between the Church and the recovery world using both the Bible and recovery literature (to set people free from addiction and provide an encounter with Jesus.) This much-needed ministry is doing truly remarkable work. "Recovery Church His Story" chronicles what God is doing and how you can join this movement. This book is a must-read for every church leader, clinician, addict, alcoholic, and anyone impacted by addiction. This book will inspire and move you to be a part of the solution."

- Paul Meier M.D. Co-Founder and Medical Director of Meier Clinics.

The word movement is radically appropriate for what is happening through Recovery Church! This is a move of God that goes beyond any plan, program, or project. The Recovery Church Movement is such a beautiful expression of how God is bringing his kingdom to life in our midst through his people. And what's fascinating about this movement is best expressed in Joshua 3:4 "...you have never been this way before." What we are seeing with Recovery Church is a new way for the gospel to advance in the new cultural landscape of our time. And it is nothing less than wondrous! Give yourself the gift of their story by taking time to read this book and allowing God to possibly meet you in a way you have never been before.

- Dr. Casey Cleveland. Lead Pastor The Avenue Church. Delray Beach, FL.

We have been excited to see the transforming power of Christ on display in the lives of people who many have written off as hopeless. We are reminded week by week that God is in the business of making all things and, therefore, all people new. We love having a recovery church in Nashville and are so grateful for the opportunity our church has to partner with this ministry. I'm excited for you to be able to read all of the stories of transformation.

- Dr. Jeff Mims. Pastor Judson Baptist Church. Nashville, TN

When first approached about the idea of Recovery Church, I had no idea what God was going to do. I just knew that the people struggling with addiction in Delray Beach needed the message of grace through our Savior, Jesus Christ. They needed the strength and healing that only Jesus can offer. Recovery Church had a vision and a plan for making that happen. They asked me if they could rent the sanctuary at Trinity for a Monday night service. I felt right away that God was going to be using this ministry to bring people to Him. I learned a long time ago to jump on board when God wants to do something. I felt honored that He was giving me and Trinity an opportunity to make even a small difference. I told Mitch that Recovery Church could use Trinity's facilities without cost. That would be our investment in what God was going to do. Through that investment and the investments of so many others, God has done amazing things. I am in awe of what God is doing every week to bring salvation, healing, and recovery through the Recovery Church Movement. Praise God and thank you to all who have worked so hard to make Recovery Church a reality.

- Pastor Vince Putnam. Senior Pastor of Trinity Lutheran Church and School. Delray Beach, FL

I love Recovery Church. It's one of the only places I have been where people are real about their stuff. In "regular" churches, everyone smiles and pretends everything is going great. But in Recovery Church, people say, "My name is _____ and I'm a recovering _____." Those introductions are authentic - the way that all Christians should be willing to talk to each other. A thoroughly Biblical understanding of grace should unleash a radical willingness to be real about our stuff with each other. This is the gift of Recovery Church - creating a culture of authenticity that becomes normal for those who regularly attend, and a prophetic invitation for the occasional guest.

- Rev. Dr. Shawn Allen. Senior Pastor Church in the Palms. Greenacres, FL

FOREWORD

Even though I come from generations of alcoholics who have recovered in AA, I must admit I grew up with a typical Evangelical distrust for any program that refused to specifically name the name of Jesus. It wasn't until I started to wonder about what discipleship actually was that AA started to get my attention and then admiration as I learned more. We were planting a church, meeting outside near a beach, when a lifeguard who had come to Jesus through Al-Anon joined our church, and we became (and still are) good friends. We had many, many discussions, comparing and contrasting 12-step groups with churches, in content, methods and goals. About that time is when I picked up my copy of Renovation of the Heart by Dallas Willard. And typical of Dallas, he blew my mind when I read this quote from him in Renovation:

> "The familiar means of the traditional AA program—the famous 'twelve steps' and the personal and social arrangements in which they are concretely embodied, including a conscious involvement of God in the individual's life—are highly effective in bringing about personal transformation. Historically, the AA program was closely aligned with the church and Christian traditions, and now it has much to give back to the church that has largely lost its grip on spiritual formation as a standard path of Christian life. Any successful plan for spiritual formation, whether for the individual or group, will in fact be significantly similar to the *Alcoholics Anonymous program*." (emphasis in original)

It would be one thing to read that from someone who was a relative newbie (as I was) to matters of the spiritual disciplines and spiritual formation. But to read that from Dallas, I was floored. Still am. And I was increasingly convinced by Dallas and the gospels that the AA program was significantly aligned with Jesus' specific ideas about the gospel and the process of transformation and participation it invites. At that point, I was determined to study (and personally work) not just the steps but also the "personal and social arrangements" of AA. So, I read Alcoholics Anonymous (i.e., the "Big Book") as well as Twelve Steps and Twelve Traditions and a variety of other materials, all of which I recommend. But most importantly, I decided to work the steps.

What I discovered fairly quickly is that the steps are not meant to be worked alone. I doubt they can be worked alone. At least, I couldn't do it. They're hard. Or, to put it another way, the sin within me is much harder to see, grab and wrestle out the door than I realized. Or, to put it another way still, it's hard to crucify one's self by one's self. Frustration and pain were easy to accomplish alone, but not working the steps. Those "personal and social arrangements" Dallas mentioned were not fluff but a necessary part of the program. It is these "personal and social arrangements"—the content and shape of certain relationships that are encouraged in recovery—that are often the hidden key to the program and are so critical in Recovery Churches. When working the steps, I needed the help of another person. Almost everyone needs help, preferably from someone who has walked the path before and who has faced the depths of their own junk with as much honesty and grace as they could find and continues to face it as it arises, someone who now has the kind of humbly honest and gracious connection with God, themselves and others that we'd like to have—and the peace that comes with it.

In 12-step groups generally, including at Recovery Church, that someone is called a sponsor. Much can be said about this, but for now, I'll just quote from the introductory section of the AA pamphlet on sponsors: "sponsor and sponsored meet as equals[.] Essentially, the process of sponsorship is this: An alcoholic who has made some progress in the recovery program shares that experience on a continuous, individual basis with another alcoholic who is attempting to attain or maintain sobriety." Encouraging and practicing this kind of voluntary yet deep, one on one relationship is a foundational part of recovery. If there is an anti-Cain (of Cain and Able fame), it is the sponsor. Sponsors are there to support and help the sponsored make progress, but as an equal, a brother. They are a flesh and blood relational lifeline for the person who needs an experienced brother or sister on the walk of real honesty and change. I'm reminded how Jesus sent his disciples out in pairs and how (thankfully) more and more pastors and others in ministry are seeking out a spiritual director. When it comes to really dealing with our own issues, those in recovery have long recognized the need for a wise and experienced friend. Not a boss, but someone who has walked the path and is willing to walk with us in ours.

In addition to getting a sponsor, who is often available for calls at virtually any hour, the newcomer to recovery (and at Recovery Church) is often encouraged to attend 90 meetings in 90 days. Think about that for a moment. Several things came to my mind when I first heard that: My first thought was an impressed form of shock: *There are actually enough AA groups in most places that 90 in 90 is possible!?* And my second reaction to the 90 in 90 was back to Dallas and how I was learning that spiritual formation works communally: *Talk about community immersion . . . wow!* If the goal is transformation of people, then 90 in 90 for the person who's ready for change makes perfect sense. This is why Recovery Churches are not in competition with each other, or with other churches, or with other recovery meetings. This is why every Recovery Church has a table with lists of nearby NA meetings, AA meetings, churches, and more. This is why Recovery Churches in the same area try to meet on different days from each other. If you go to a Recovery Church meeting in Lake Worth on Thursday, you're likely to see some of the same folks if you go to Recovery Church Delray on Monday. We're in the transformation business, and for that work, getting together once or twice a week won't cut it. *Immersion* into a new community is key.

But community and its (trans)formative power is a two-way street. "Bad company corrupts good character" is the way the New Testament sums up the problem when one's community is headed in problematic directions. And for many in the Church, the jury is still out regarding the folks who regularly fill the pews (and the pulpits!). At Recovery Churches almost everyone at Recovery Church is an alcoholic or some other kind of addict in various stages of recovery. Smoking outside the sanctuary just before or after a Recovery Church meeting is a given for a good percentage of the congregation. Meeting speakers talk openly about the death, destruction, and crime that addiction produced in and around them and occasionally do so with colorful language. As a result, some have asked me, as a father of teens and an 8-year-old, if I'm okay with my kids attending Recovery Church with me, concerned about the influence.

To that concern, I'll give a story. When I first took my whole family with me to a Recovery Church meeting, we happened to come on a monthly "anniversary night." As this part of the service began, the MC announced they were going to give out crosses to commemorate and celebrate people at different milestones in recovery, which is similar to giving chips in AA. The first, he said, was a cross for those who were "sick and tired of being sick and tired." Maybe such folks were at step one or just headed in that direction, but it was clear that by walking up and getting that cross, folks were saying they at least wanted a change; they wanted sobriety. As four or five people stood up, the place erupted in cheers, shouts, and applause. As each one picked up their cross at the front, the few folks handing out crosses were embracing those that came up. A few more came up. The applause and shouts never stopped, just increased when another stood up and walked to pick up their cross and be embraced. After ten or so got this first cross, the MC then asked, "How many at one month?" One month sober. The crowd's cheers had let up for just a bit for the MC, whom we could barely hear, even though he had a mic, but then erupted again as people rose to get their one-month cross, embraced by the crowd and by the people giving the crosses away.

My children watched and applauded too, becoming viscerally aware of the significance of what these milestones meant to those walking up and to the crowd. The MC then asked for folks at 90 days. And the church let loose again with shouts. "YEEAAAAAAAAHHH!" Just so proud, so encouraging. It kept going as the MC asked for a year. Then again, at multiple years. More celebration, more elation, more embraces. As it started to die down, he asked again if anyone wanted pick up that first cross, for anyone who just wants to begin, again or for the first time. A couple more came forward. The crowd got a second wind as the last few picked up their cross. Fast forward to the end of the service, my wife, as a long-time charismatic, said, "That's the most I've experienced the presence of the Holy Spirit in a while," and as folks started to filter out, my 14-year-old asked me, "Can you introduce me to some of these awesome people?" My oldest just sat there, clearly affected by the service. She still can't really articulate it. She just smiles and says, "Something happened" to her as she took it all in and just said repeatedly how real the people were. It might have been just another day for my eight-year-old, to be honest; we'll have to see. But for me, I was reminded of how heaven rejoices when just one sinner repents. Being surrounded by these shouts and applause and joy for people picking up their crosses might have been the closest to heaven I've ever been, and I'm thrilled for my kids to be here with me, with people who feel and act so much like heaven.

What you just read is an example of something that Recovery Church has learned from AA, and it is key to understanding Recovery Church and this book. In actuality, it's a value and practice that, like the bulk of the program, AA learned first from the Church. Recovery Church is big on *personal stories* or what we in the Church might call *testimonies*. If you spend any length of time going to any support group meetings, you will hear an abundance of personal stories of failure and progress. These stories are not only disarming because of their honesty about real failures in a way that is uncommon. They are magnetic.

The practice of such honesty, of being real (what we at Recovery Churches often sum up as being "raw"), makes both the program and the recovery group very attractive for those just considering recovery, especially when the stories of failure outstrip the failures of the newcomer! Just hearing other addicts be honest about their lives without being shamed crushes one of the biggest lies standing in the way of any recovery, namely, *if I allow anyone—even myself—to really look at and know the truth of what I am and have done, I will be, and should be, shamed to death.* The honest testimonies we hear regularly at Recovery Church and in recovery meetings around the world *destroy* this poisonous and untrue belief. It's God's grace that makes it untrue, and our stories make this grace a concrete reality for people to see and grab hold of. They are a profound and powerful spiritual weapon for tearing down the strongholds of addiction and shame. Further, because there are often blessings and redemption on the other side of failure in these stories, the stories give *hope*, which is essential to taking a new path. There has to be hope that this community, these steps, this Jesus, leads somewhere good.

That is why the bulk of this book, like so many Recovery Church meetings, is made up stories of what God has done for people. As you read them, I hope they do for you what they do for all of us. As you read this book, you'll take in stories of failure and success from real folks who have hopefully gotten closer to death and destruction than you have. But you will see God and his people still meeting them there. You will see people facing the truth about themselves, asking for help, and getting it. I hope these stories do for you what they do for so many of us. I hope they do for you what they do for so many addicts who continue to come to Recovery Church for the first time, just wondering if recovery—if real change—is even possible for them:

They begin to believe.

T Freeman
North Palm Beach, FL

DEDICATION

This book is dedicated to all those who have been impacted by the deadly struggle of alcoholism and addiction: to those who are currently suffering, to those who have lost the fight, and the families who have lost those they love. May this book offer a path of healing and hope. This is not a disease of "those people." It is us. We have 12-Steps, but 1 Goal.

ACKNOWLEDGMENTS

"If I have seen further, it is by standing on the shoulders of Giants."
— Isaac Newton.

Anything good found in the Recovery Church Movement is there because of countless people who laid a foundation before us. Frankly, we have no idea what we're doing. We are simply attempting to take the next faithful steps on a path that has been unfolding before us. The sacrifice of countless others has trodden this path. The Christian faith is built upon sacrifice of oneself for others.

There is no greater love than this: that a person would lay down his life for the sake of his friends. — Jesus

Recovery Church exists today because of this pattern of sacrificial surrender. From the saints who followed Christ to their death, to the mavericks of recovery who chose to be "responsible. When anyone, anywhere, reached out for help..." – A.A, to people across the country who have caught the vision and sacrificially given. Recovery Church says, "Thank you!"

CONTENTS

His Story
The Beginning

All great stories start with a great beginning. And the greatest story ever told, God's story, starts with the greatest beginning imaginable. "In the beginning, God…" (Genesis 1:1 NIV). It all starts with Him. "In the beginning, God created" (Genesis 1:1 NIV). With a word, He created the heavens, created the earth, and created us. I love how God is so powerful that with His word, he created everything we can see and touch. God said, "Let there be," and it was so, and it was good. With a word, "Let there be light," and there was light, and it was good. How powerful is the Word of God? Powerful enough to be the foundation of everything we know.

The creation story takes an unusual turn. God said, let there be, it was so, and it was good. Over and over again, until us. When the story of God tells our story, something changes in this pattern and maybe even tone. It's almost as if God pauses as he reflects on all the beauty (the great ocean depths, the snow-capped mountain peaks, the sun and stars, the atom, DNA, from the smallest detail to the breathtaking splendor) and it's as if he says, "Hmm, I know what is missing to make this just the way it should be." "So, God created man in his own image, in the image of God he created him; male and female he created them" (Genesis 1:27 ESV). God could have just said, "Let there be man." However, "the LORD God formed the man from the dust of the ground and breathed into his nostrils the breath of life, and the man became a living being" (Genesis 2:7 NIV).

It's almost as if I can see God stepping down from heaven, reaching into the dirt, finding the perfect piece of clay, and molding us into exactly who he wanted to create. Then, gently laying his fragile creation down, kneeling, pressing his lips to ours, and breathing His life into us. What an intimate, powerful scene. Like a parent holding their precious newborn baby for the first time, He looks at His creation and now says, "It is very good" (Genesis 1:31 NIV). But we know the story doesn't end there with this beautiful scene. Sin enters the picture and begins to mar His masterpiece. Over time this corruption spreads. However, God is the perfect father and has a solution to help His creation recover. A solution that might seem foolish to many. A solution found through the birth of His son, His death on the cross, and rising from the dead. A solution that is not found inside an individual, in their own will. But a solution that is found in total surrender of their will back to the beginning, God.

This beautiful mess we call Recovery Church is no different. It all starts with Him and His children finding their way back to Him. It is impossible to tell the story of how God authored Recovery Church without beginning with the stories of the people of Recovery Church. The Holy Spirit was writing the vision of Recovery Church on the hearts of strangers from across this country and then brought this rag-tag group together into a family. The story of Recovery Church is His Story. The story of how a Holy God went through extravagant measures to reach the junkie, drunk, crackhead, outcasts, sinners, wayward children, the lepers of today- us. From physicians, ministers, teachers, fathers, mothers, sons, daughters, homeless, affluent, poor, from every race, our growing fellowship is united in our shared solution through Jesus.

Phil's Story
The Reluctant Leader

To tell His Story of Recovery Church, I reluctantly need to start with His Story of how I came to be a part of this amazing, beautiful mess we call Recovery Church. I say reluctantly because Recovery Church is not my story; it is His Story, and I'm just grateful God has allowed me to be part of how He has decided to build His Church. However, I don't know how to share this story without sharing how He transformed me. The story is much more miraculous and more significant than any one person's story, especially mine. God used Recovery Church to save and transform thousands, and I'm one of those people. A sinner in need of a savior, and that Savior is Jesus. Here is His Story of Recovery Church.

In the 1990's I found myself spiritually lost. I was seeking acceptance on the beaches of Daytona Beach during the heyday of the "MTV Spring Break" era. With the backdrop of wet t-shirt contests, nightclubs, partying spring breakers, and sex, I was an awkward, nervous, adolescent of the world, being pulled further into the world but at the same time being deeply drawn into a relationship with Jesus. I fully believe I fell in love with Jesus, my savior, during this time but also fell in love with this thing called "liquid courage." I first found the bottle around sixth grade. Depression and suicidal thoughts began to infiltrate my world. I always was a bit of an outsider, never really found my place. I found this strange solution through the bottle. By the time high school rolled around an occasional mudslide in my coffee thermos during my homeroom class would give me enough courage to make it through my morning classes. Then slowly, this "spirit" began to get its hooks into my soul. I made the decision that I needed to go to a christian university. I sincerely wanted to go to a place where there would be people further along in their christian walk, and I was afraid that if I went to a secular school, I would become like my older brother, "a real alcoholic." I had this strange fear that if I went to a "party school," I would not live to see my graduation.

However, I didn't see myself as one of "those" people. I drank because it helped me feel like I fit in. I was just a partier and a sloppy one at that. I was not under the bridge, I was an honor student, hardworking, and if you asked my family or many at my newfound church, I was a "good kid." I was "bud" or "buddy," disarming, awkward, but very few would have recognized I had a problem. Especially me. You see, my brother Kevin was ten years older, and my brokenness could hide in the shadow of his destruction. It was apparent to all around him that he had a problem. He started using around eleven years old and the wreckage was everywhere. So, he had over a decade head start on me. From my perspective, my problems always paled in comparison.

As naive as it might sound, I genuinely went off to that christian school hoping to find people who could help guide and mentor me to mature in my faith and life. However, when I arrived, I was met by kids who were just now having a bit of freedom. They wanted to go to the clubs for the first time, party, and have a bit of "college adventure." I so deeply needed to be accepted and my drinking quickly progressed. Yet at the same time, I was falling deeper in love with Jesus. I know that might not make sense to some who read this. How could he be falling deeper into sin and at the same time falling deeper in love with Jesus?

I was raised in a good family of the world, where church was something good people did, but not so much my family. Born in the late '70s, I was a child of a hardworking family, public schools, and 80s/90s tv. The world had its grasp on me, yet not in an overtly dark way, but in more subtle appealing ways. Yes, there were plenty of wounds and brokenness, but I drank "essentially because I liked the effect produced by alcohol. The sensation was so elusive that, while I admitted it caused me problems, I could not after a time differentiate the true from the false. To me, my alcoholic life seemed the only normal one." (Paraphrased from the Doctor's Opinion — Alcoholics Anonymous). If you would have asked me at this time in my story, "Are you an alcoholic?" I would have felt it was the most ridiculous question you could have asked and laughed it off. I had no insight into the path I was traversing. Sometime in the late 90s, while at this school, I found myself befriended by a young youth pastor. I was hired as the assistant youth pastor, yet my drinking continued to progress.

A pivotal moment in my story took place during this season. Once a week, I led an early morning Bible study for middle school students who wanted to grow in their faith. These students would arrive at school an hour earlier than everyone else to study God's word, and it was my job to lead them. However, this day was different. The night before, a group of friends and I left our dorm rooms and went out drinking. Most drank enough to feel a bit tipsy and then stopped to return to campus. However, I never understood "tipsy;" instead, I drank to get drunk. So slowly, one by one, as the night progressed, our numbers decreased as others stopped drinking and returned to the dorms. Our school was a "dry" campus, so if I showed back up on campus intoxicated I would risk being expelled. So, I kept drinking. Sometime during the night, I remembered I needed to be at church early the following morning. I was met with this conundrum. If I stopped drinking, I would risk falling asleep, and I knew I would not wake up in time to lead the middle school student Bible study. I decided to keep drinking to avoid disappointing those students. Great idea, I know (sarcastic if you couldn't tell).

Fully intoxicated, I made my way to the church. I walked up the stairs to the youth room to find a group of a dozen or so students already sitting in a circle waiting for me to teach them. The next memory I have is of a garbage can placed between my legs, being held by a middle school girl, and me uncontrollably vomiting. When I raised my head, I made eye contact with this young girl and saw tears running down her face. She knew what I didn't know. She had smelled that smell before. I had counseled her in the past because her mother was an alcoholic. At that moment, I quit! I knew I couldn't be a hypocrite. I knew I couldn't be a minister and drink this way. So, I quit! I did not quit drinking. I quit the ministry.

Over time, a ministry mentor and friend walked alongside me and helped me. However, something was missing. I saw my drinking simply as a wrong choice, a mistake, a moral failing. Yes, it was all those things and more. I didn't yet see myself as having a problem with alcohol. I had this reservation in the back of my mind that I could eventually learn to "drink like a gentleman." I was a new creation in Christ. I had the freedom to drink, right? A few years passed. I was newly married and fresh out of graduate school when I took a call as a youth pastor at another church.

This church came from a tradition without many restrictions on drinking. They had an outreach called "Theology on Tap" modeled after Martin Luther, where they met in a local pub and hosted conversations around faith. Drinking, at times, was just an acceptable part of their culture. After a few months at this church, the senior pastor invited me to give the Sunday evening message for the first time. I prepared and prepared. I was overwhelmingly nervous. Sunday afternoon came, and some of the leadership saw how nervous I was. After praying for me, they suggested, "Let's go to Thirsty Turtle and take the edge off." Thirsty Turtle was a local bar and grill down the road. "What'll you have?" They ordered beer and I ordered a rum and coke. And another. And another. After the third rum and coke, the pastor with me said something to the effect of "I think that's enough." So, I proceeded to preach my first sermon under the influence. As I shared that evening, I began to break out in hives. I'm not talking about a little rash; I'm talking about eyes swelling shut, tongue swelling, hives! Hives so extreme that a nurse in the congregation walked to the front of the room and gave me a cup of water and a Benadryl.

Leaving that service, I walked outside, and a treatment center van arrived. We hosted a local A.A. meeting in the youth room every Sunday evening. Sitting at the picnic tables, with a cloud of smoke, was a familiar face from years before. It was that middle school girl who held the garbage can, who knew I had a problem with alcohol before I knew I had a problem with alcohol. She was a young woman now and attending that A.A. meeting. A "normal" person might get the hint that God seemed to be shouting. Minimally, they may have concluded that it was not wise for them to drink. God had literally given me an allergy to alcohol, so maybe I should listen. But not me. Now I felt like I had the church's permission, and I could just take a Benadryl while I drank, and as long as I wasn't too intoxicated at church events, it would be ok.

Again, during this season, most would not have seen my problems with alcohol as severe. I was reliable, hardworking, and we saw some fruit in this ministry. But, under the surface, things were getting dark, yet again. I remember one evening looking my new bride in her eyes and seeing what I interpreted as a mixture of regret and fear. It was as if her eyes were saying, "Did I just make the worst mistake in my life? What is my future going to look like down this path?" Then I had a great gift from God, a moment of clarity. A moment where God let me see that no matter how much of a new creation I became, it became clear that it would never be wise for me to drink again.

Fast forward a few years. I found recovery, worked a program of recovery, helped start a church and was later hired to help treatment centers establish Christian programs within secular facilities. One afternoon a young lady, whom I'll call Rachel, a "frequent flyer" at our facility, was sitting awaiting her intake into treatment yet again. Rachel was a sweet girl about nineteen years old, and we loved her at the facility. As I sat at my desk, watching through the open doorway, I could see her waiting in the lobby for the behavioral health technician to complete her intake. She seemed so defeated, hopeless, and broken, coming to this treatment center yet again, hoping she'd find a solution to the insanity. The Holy Spirit began to swell up inside me, saying, "Tell her about me," "Tell her about Jesus." As I began to stand up from my desk, suddenly another patient in the lobby collapsed and fell to the ground with chest pains. After he had been transferred to the emergency room and the chaos passed, I finished out my day. Exhausted, I was ready to head home.

During the drive home, it hit me, "I never shared with Rachel about Jesus. God forgive me! Ok, Lord, I'll tell her first thing tomorrow." That night, in the middle of the night, I awoke to my phone ringing incessantly. The behavioral health technician had found Rachel dead in a closet from an overdose. Rachel was my first death in this way, and there would be hundreds more to come. Over the next few days, I made a couple of promises to God. Any ministry I was a part of was going to do two things: (1) Allow people multiple opportunities to hear the Gospel and fall in love with Jesus and (2) Help those struggling with addiction find a path of recovery.

Around 2011, I was recruited by a growing secular addictions treatment facility to establish a Christian program within their institution. This time, I would place those two promises at the center of anything we did. During this season, God began to piece together a team. Upon arrival, I found God had already placed some faithful followers of Christ who were serving on the front lines of an epidemic. They were sacrificially loving on addicts and alcoholics. They were doing everything in their power to allow people to find Jesus and recovery. One of those men was the Medical Director, Dr. "B." He really was an evangelist who just happened to be a great physician in his downtime. On my first day, he invited me into his exam room, where he proceeded to invite a patient to kneel, pray to accept

Jesus, and then began renouncing demonic strongholds. I had never had a first day on the job quite like this one.

Dr. B. was a force devoted to Jesus like no one I had ever met. So, Dr. B., Father Ron (a catholic monsignor), myself, and too many others to be named started a church service in the middle of this secular facility, in the middle of the clinical week. We said we were going to place "disputable matters" aside and focus on Jesus and Recovery, and that is what we did.

I remember when I realized that so many in our care had never really heard the Gospel. At a Good Friday service, we shared the Passion story of Jesus and a young lady deeply moved yelled from her seat, "They aren't going to kill him, are they?!" She had never heard God's story of salvation through Jesus. We were given this sacred opportunity to share the Gospel with her and countless others. We could fill volumes with God's divine, miraculous, often heart-wrenching and astonishing work. Working on the front lines of addiction is the front line of spiritual battles that words really cannot fully convey. This list of people God raised up to help serve during this time could feel like reading a Biblical genealogy; I'll spare you an exhaustive list. Many are still ministering today. From Pastor Mike, Patrick, John, Dan, Louis, Bernard, James, Tara, Rachel, Lyndsey…. It was truly amazing how God grew this team.

The church service quickly became one of the favorite groups at the facility. Week in and week out, dozens of people would pray to surrender to Jesus. The patients began to call the service "Drunk Church" and even came up with a slogan. "You may have been to church drunk, but you've never been to Drunk Church." Every week we would take at least one, sometimes as many as three, full fifteen passenger vans, to the beach or local churches for dozens to be baptized. On all metrics, those participating in the Christian program were measurably more successful (length of stay, completion of care, fewer behavioral issues, lower recidivism, etc.).

One of the owners of the facility was "a man of peace" but not a follower of Jesus. He had witnessed what was happening and was beyond intrigued. Bill invited me into his office and said, "Pastor Phil, when I bless you, I seem to be blessed. Is that strange?" "No, Bill, that's not strange at all; please keep blessing me ☺." "Well, Pastor Phil, I know you believe it's Jesus, but I think it might be spirits. However, whatever is out there, seems to be telling me that you need to start a church for addicts and alcoholics. Do you think this is a good idea?" he asked. "Bill, you know, yes, maybe, umm, I'm really not sure." And honestly, I wasn't sure. I was so conflicted. Excited on the one hand but unsure on the other. I had no concerns for our little gathering in a treatment center, but for some reason, the idea of a church outside the walls focused on those who struggle with addiction seemed absurd. At first, theologically, I grappled with the concept of a church created around addiction. However, so many were dying without Jesus. Something had to be done. But was it a realistic idea? I had helped plant churches in the past, and it was some of the most challenging work I had done. Now, he thinks it's a good idea to add the layer of people early in recovery? The proposal seemed utterly insane.

At the same time, Pastor David, a conservative Baptist pastor of a local megachurch, was relentlessly asking me to help him with the recovery ministry of his church. He had attempted another ministry to addicts and alcoholics but felt something was missing and believed God was leading him to activate me to do this. Like I needed one more thing on my already full plate. My family was growing, the job was intense, hundreds were coming to faith, and many were being rescued from the bondage of addiction. Yet still, many were dying. Time was short. I had a full, busy life, and I didn't feel I had the margin for one more thing. "Planting a church is possibly the loneliest, hardest thing on the planet" (Rick Warren, Founding Pastor of

Saddleback Church). I didn't have room for another ministry, and no way I was going to start another church, let alone a church for addicts and alcoholics. I just couldn't imagine how hard that would be. So, I had an idea. How about I get my boss together with this Baptist pastor? Frankly, I was kind of hoping that they would meet and decide, "No, this is not a good idea." Maybe David would share the Gospel with my boss. Maybe he'd come to faith in Jesus. But certainly, I wasn't going to be starting a church for addicts and alcoholics. Certainly, they would say no for me.

Well, I was completely wrong. They both thought it was the best idea ever and I needed to be the one to do it. The secular treatment center was going to allow me, and any of my team members, to volunteer our time while on the clock to start this church. In fact, this secular facility was going to partner with David's church to see this church started. So, while I was a little scared, it appeared evident God was orchestrating the start of this new Church. So, we started with no vision besides helping some addicts and alcoholics in south Florida find Jesus and Recovery.

Stumbling and fumbling, we started to gather with the focus of giving them Jesus and Recovery. We followed the model we learned in that treatment center; a time of worship, a message connecting scriptures to recovery principles, a time of surrender, and an opportunity for transparent sharing. After a few moves, Recovery Church was born, and we found ourselves in Lake Worth, Florida. Lake Worth Beach is a small community within the South Florida metropolis. In redevelopment, Lake Worth is a bit eclectic, filled with artists, progressive, and a little raw. We started meeting in a run-down coffee shop, where rumor had it the previous tenant might have been selling "more than coffee" from the back. The AC was broken more often than not. But God showed up. Without any promotion, that little coffee shop, which could comfortably seat twenty-five people, had well over one hundred crammed inside, standing in the windows, out to the street, trying to find a way into the building. We had to start limiting the number of people who could enter the building. We placed speakers outside on the sidewalk so those in the street unable to physically fit in the building could still hear.

To us, this event felt like a scene out of the book of Acts. I can remember one night preparing for baptisms, cleaning the alley behind the coffee shop, blowing up a "kiddie pool" (having to remove needles, spoons, and condoms to set up), and a line of new believers waiting to be baptized. A short time later, we knew we needed more space. God started stirring in us a little more faith and a little more vision. So, we stood in that street and prayed. As we looked up from that prayer, my eyes caught the sign of the Bamboo Room across the street. The Bamboo Room is an iconic nightclub with leopard carpet, bamboo-covered walls, and a giant moose head on the wall. The floors still a bit sticky from nearly a century of serving alcohol, our fledgling church of people early in their faith and recovery moved into a bar! I know, I know; I shake my head even as I write these words. However, God's favor was so palatable. We kept taking the next uncomfortable steps, and people kept coming, surrendering to Jesus, and finding a path of recovery. We were thrilled, overwhelmed, and amazed by everything God did during these early years. The sheer numbers that came to faith and were baptized were mind-boggling at times. But something happened. We became comfortable. As the A.A. *Big Book* says, we began to "rest on our laurels." Why would we change anything? It was working, and that was as far as our vision went.

I don't want to paint a rose-colored glasses picture here. Being one of the "Drunk Church Pastors" was hard, really hard, and by far the most challenging work I have ever been a part of. The entire team went through the wringer at times. There were spiritual attacks, physical attacks, death threats, stalkers, deaths and relapses. Anything you could think of, we probably saw during this time. Rarely a week passed during this season when someone we knew didn't die. But there was also so much beauty. Lives were transformed, families restored, eternities changed. I believe that God was throwing parties with us in heaven as He saw His children return to Him. He was brought joy as He saw His creation begin to be restored. As the years started to pass, the treatment center closed, Pastor David left his church, some of our initial team moved on, some died, and a couple even left the faith, but Recovery Church remained.

South Florida is a bit transient, particularly the recovery community. Our fellowship was almost always in flux. People would leave south Florida and return "home" to Tennessee, New Jersey, all over the country and reach back out to us. Many would say something to the effect, "I need Recovery Church. Any chance you are willing to open a Recovery Church here?" Being the reluctant leader I am, with a plate that was overflowing, my response was, "I'm sorry, but no." Then Wayne, George, and a group started traveling three hours round trip to be a part of our fellowship. I saw the insanity of this, and George asked, "any chance you would be willing to start a Recovery Church in Vero Beach?" Without really thinking, my response changed, "No, I can't, but I can help you do it." With that statement, RC went from that one mission outpost to two and then three locations.

Pastor David founded this international church planting organization called The Timothy Initiative and offered me a job as their Chief Operations Officer. It was great and certainly a lot less hectic than the treatment world. Recovery Church was this exciting hobby on the side, and I got paid to help behind the scenes of this growing organization to plant churches around the world. Then sometime later I got the call that we needed to relocate our offices to Raleigh, North Carolina. This meant that with five kids, the youngest only eight weeks old, still in boxes from just moving, we would need to repack and move yet again. Something strange was happening inside of me. I was fine with moving to Raleigh (I didn't like the timing, but I was willing and started looking at houses). However, I had this almost overwhelming grief at the thought of leaving Recovery Church. Not that Recovery Church needed me. God proved to me that RC was bigger than me. I certainly had enough faith now to believe it would outlive me, but the thought of leaving Recovery Church broke my heart. This fellowship radically changed me, made me a better husband, father, and leader, and I needed it.

That Friday, I began praying, but God wouldn't release me from Recovery Church. I argued with God, "God, I have a great job; just let me let go of this stupid hobby." He responded, "Just tell them the vision I gave you for RC." I questioned, "God, what are you talking about? God, are you crazy?" He responded, "Just tell them the vision I gave you." I doubted, "God, you really want churches *for* people in recovery and *by* people in recovery? God, this is crazy! Do you know how messy this is going to be?" He responded, "Just tell them the vision." "Ok, I will, but this is going to be a mess." I finished the prayer (sometimes my prayers seem like an adolescent arguing with their parent) when the phone immediately began to ring. It was a pastor acquaintance about five hours away. He had just returned from a trip to Cambodia and had a bit of a stomach bug. He said, "Phil, I'll be at church on Sunday, but I'm not 100%. I might need to leave the room during the service. Could you come this Sunday and just share the vision God has given you for Recovery Church?"

The next day I hit the road, leaving my wife home with an infant, packed boxes, and three other kids. I took our rambunctious toddler with me. Yes, we have five kids, and yes, I left four of them with my wife who had recently delivered our youngest. And yes, we had only recently moved into this house, a fixer-upper "new to us" house filled with boxes. Please, send my wife a gift; she deserves it. I think she just might have one of the most challenging jobs around.

That Sunday, for two services, I shared the story of RC and the vision I didn't fully yet believe myself. The pastor took me aside and said something to the effect, "I know there are some people here who have been impacted by addiction, but I'm really not sure if it's that many." So, I shared stories of how God rescued people from the bondage of addiction and how he used them to be his hands and minister to others in the most remarkable ways. I shared stats on how bad the crisis was in our land. The number one cause of death in our nation for people under the age of fifty was an overdose. Your child is more likely to die from an overdose than any other cause of death. The utter insanity of this thing we call addiction. As I was preaching, I debated in my head, "God am I getting too graphic? Are these people hearing this? Should I change the message?" But God said, "keep sharing the vision." So, I shared the vision. A movement across this nation led by people in recovery, a movement of God, that transforms this land for him, with former addicts and alcoholics leading the charge. Where it's so undeniable that God is the one leading because how else could you explain a church of former addicts and alcoholics changing this nation, "but God."

The first service was a bit of an older crowd. When I finished teaching, we invited anyone who needed prayer to come forward, and I would pray with them—a line of hurting people formed from the front to the back of the church. Grandparents asked for prayers as they were raising their grandchildren. The parents of their grandchildren had either died, were in active addiction, or were in institutions. We had to cut the prayer time off as the next service was starting. Near the back of the room, a lady from the first service stayed for the second service. I preached, and again after I finished, we offered a time of prayer. This time it was a bit younger of a crowd and more people who were admitting their struggles. After an extended prayer time, the woman who stayed for the first service approached me. She asked me a question. "Pastor Phil, how can I help you do what God has called you to do?" You know, in that moment, I still didn't fully believe the vision God had given me. I was still planning on the move to North Carolina. I was only willing to be obedient to just "share the vision." After trying to answer her questions with all the "right" answers, i.e., pray for us, pray for God's protection, etc., these words popped out of me without thinking, "Are you talking about money?" If you know me, that is not like me. But her response was "Yes."

I really hadn't accepted the call on my life to do this full-time; I mean who wants to grow up and be known as "The Drunk Church Pastor." I wanted to be a "real" leader of the faith, not this "side show." I was just willing to share the vision. I got lost in the weeds a bit with her by attempting to explain the Great Commission Fund of my denomination and other possible options of how she could donate. I told her to talk to the pastor of the church, as I was a guest. We would see if he could take the check, and I'd work something out with him to make sure it was used wisely to reach addicts and alcoholics. She wasn't having it. She said something to the effect, "I do not know anything about this Christian and Missionary Alliance, the Great Commission Fund, or even this church. You see, I was driving down the road on the way to my church and felt God tell me to come in here today. Now I know why. I feel led to help you fulfill this vision". Still, the hard-headed reluctant leader I am, I asked her to please honor the local pastor and ask him for his blessing. She did, but shortly after that, she returned with the pastor. He said to me, "Phil, any reason you just can't take the check from her?" So, I received this check for Recovery Church. Thanking her, I finished praying with a few people and hit the road to return home.

On the drive home, my curiosity got the best of me. I had to see how much the check was. God was undoubtedly moving, but God, "why won't you just release me from RC?" I unfolded the check to see it was for $10,000.00. "God, who gives a stranger a check for ten thousand dollars?" "God, what am I going to do with $10,000.00? It's a lot of money, but not enough to fulfill your vision." On that drive, I prayed and felt led to reach out to my boss. "David, I need to tell you what God is doing". I told him of this lady's gift. I told him of how God just wouldn't release me from RC, and he responded, "You're not coming to Raleigh, are you?" "Well, I really don't know…" "No," David said, "Phil, you're not coming to Raleigh. Doesn't it seem clear, that God has a call on you that seems obvious, and don't you think you need to listen?" The conversation ensued, and David explained that a generous church in Virginia would provide my family with health insurance and TTI would provide my salary for the next six months. That if I could raise another $20,000.00, they would match the $30,000.00 so we could start the ministry with health insurance and $60,000.00. As I hung up that call and continued the drive, I realized something, "Did God just have me quit, or was I just fired from my job to fulfill this vision?" "Oh boy. How do I explain this to my wife, Sara?"

We hit the ground running. God provided the money; we worked some behind-the-scenes organizational stuff and started "building the plane as we flew." We began saying yes to starting churches *for* people in recovery *by* people in recovery, and I began to embrace being known as the "Drunk Church Pastor." We went from three locations to four, to six, to ten, to fifteen to eighteen locations, all within two years. Some people thought I was nuts and even called me a heretic and other colorful names. But too many people were dying without knowing Jesus and a path of recovery. We just had to keep moving forward.

Then the world changed in 2020. Like everyone, we didn't know what to expect. However, we believed isolation could kill our community faster than a pandemic. We pivoted and opened daily online services and zoom meetings. We knew these were great tools but not the long-term solution for our entire community. As soon as we could, one by one, our locations began to gather again, but not without cost from the pandemic

(Dear friends died from Covid, including Dr. B.). However, many more were dying from the isolation, suicides, and overdoses that wreaked havoc on the recovery community. We kept pushing forward and kept planting. Throughout the pandemic, we kept saying yes and kept seeing little churches spring up. Some didn't make it, but most did, most thrived, and now thousands have heard the Gospel, and it's just the beginning.

I was a bit hesitant to share this story. Because Recovery Church is still in its infancy. We're still like that fragile creation that God so carefully laid on the ground, kneeling, pressing his lips to ours, and breathing His life into us. Is it youthful idealism or audacious faith to believe God will do this? Only time will tell that part of the story. But God has taken me from a person of little faith and vision to now a person of bold faith and a God-sized vision. A vision to see Recovery Church in every city of this nation and beyond. A vision to see redeemed addicts and alcoholics lead a revival across this land. A story so unbelievable that if it's true, it's undeniably God's story.

This movement is about God and His Story. It is about His children being rescued and empowered to be His hands and feet. His story of how He redeems what was thought lost, how He is restoring His creation to Him. A story of how God said, "Let there be…," and there was this crazy beautiful mess we call Recovery Church. I believe He is shouting from heaven, "It is so very good!" Over the following few pages, you will meet Pastor Mike, Kentucky Dave, Chrispy, Junior, Max, Janice, and many more. A family that only God could bring together. The most unlikely group to ever lead this revival, but that might just be the point. Because it's His Church, His Story, not ours.

Mike's Story
The Codependent Pastor

I was scared…possibly more scared than I had ever been in my ministry career. I had been in ministry for over thirty years. Those thirty-plus years of ministry had been principally serving among the "Sheep." In other words, I was a Christian Pastor serving primarily among people who already claimed Christ as their Savior. Until the moment I first walked into this treatment center, I had not realized how sheltered my ministry had been and exactly how vulnerable that had left me. And so, I was scared….

Several months before, my wife, Diane, and I had started attending and serving at Grace Fellowship Church in West Palm Beach, Florida. Having been a Pastor for so many years, the Lead Pastor at Grace, Dr. David Nelms, took an interest in Diane and me. We were raising support to go to Central America to serve the Lord by establishing a church planting network. However, the support raising was slow, and I needed income. Dr. Nelms is a gifted networker. He told me there was a young man he wanted me to meet. And so, after a Wednesday mid-week service, he introduced me to a tall, dark-haired young man named Phil Dvorak. Phil shared a little about his ministry as the Spiritual Care Director at a treatment center, and I shared a little about my background. I discovered that this treatment center was a drug and alcohol rehabilitation facility with a robust Christian program. I was impressed with Phil right from the start. He came across as a young man with vision, drive, and deep faith in Christ. He had an entrepreneurial spirit about him….one founded in faith.

Several months later, Phil and I were talking at church, and he basically offered me a part-time ministry position serving with him. I was to be the Outreach Pastor, and my primary function would be to represent the Christian program of the treatment center to area churches. Additionally, I would also lead one or two weekly groups and participate in leading the weekly church service at the facility we called Drunk Church.

And so, my first day on the job, I got up early, drove to the facility, prayed in my car in the parking lot because I was scared....and walked into the ministry "love of my life." Honestly, I fell in love with this ministry of serving men and women seeking recovery from addictions by calling on Jesus as their Higher Power. I found these dear men and women were wide open and vulnerable and mostly very honest about their brokenness. We had a sign-up list on our office door, and someone would sign up to speak to us with a comment like this: "I need to find God...can you help me?" Wow! If you love sharing the Gospel, this was the place to be!

Someone once asked me, "What is the difference between serving in a Church and serving people in recovery?" I responded, "When you minister in a Church, you spend most of your time trying to convince churchgoers they are not as good as they think they are, and not as spiritually strong as they think they are, but people starting the journey of recovery already know this and are ready to rebuild their lives." I found this exceptionally refreshing.

While I was working with these dear men and women, I began to discover something about myself. I was not as good as I thought I was, and I was not as spiritually strong as I thought I was. Their vulnerability provided a safe place for me to examine my own vulnerabilities for the first time in a very long time. I got a sponsor and began going through the 12-steps myself for Co-Dependency. This experience changed my life! I examined and faced how co-dependent I was and how co-dependency affected my ministry. I had been serving the Church to gain self-worth from people's affirmation. I now began serving Christ the way I should have been. Serving Christ because I love Him first and foremost.

And then came Recovery Church. Phil had been challenged by the CEO of the facility to extend the ministry of Drunk Church outside our walls. We prayed, started meeting at Grace Fellowship, and God laid it upon Phil's heart to move Recovery Church to downtown Lake Worth, Florida. This was a strategic spot because of its proximity to so many sober homes and half-way houses. And so, under Phil's leadership along with Adam, Patrick, James, Johnny, and myself, we started the very first Recovery Church in a small storefront on J Street in Lake Worth, Florida. We grew rapidly as word spread about this crazy idea of having a church service for addicts and alcoholics who were seeking Christ as their higher power. As we grew, we were seeing decisions to receive Christ as Savior almost every week! Baptisms were happening all the time. We moved from the small storefront to a coffee shop within a few weeks of opening. And soon, we were cramming around one hundred people into that coffee shop each week. And again, we were seeing decisions to receive Christ almost every service.

Then we moved into The Bamboo Room, which was formerly a well-known Jazz Club. It sat vacant for a few years before new owners began fixing it up. We saw our attendance grow to over two hundred attending weekly. The opportunities to participate in God saving lives and saving souls were overwhelming...it was and is wonderful!

The work was hard but so very rewarding. One night after a few years of ministry at the treatment center and Recovery Church, I realized something amazing....I was in the midst of the most fruitful years of ministry in my entire life. There is a principle in the book "Experiencing God" which explains that when you find where God is working, you join it. I began praising and worshipping God that He led me to a place where I could see God working in unparalleled ways and that He allowed me the privilege of joining in that work.

And that work of God through Recovery Church is still seeing the marvelous favor of God. As people completed their treatment and moved back to their homes, they started attending church. And in those churches, they began to explain to their Pastors what they had seen and experienced at Recovery Church. One by one....a few at a time...we started receiving phone calls from Pastors in New York and New Jersey, and North Florida asking if we could help them start Recovery Churches in their communities.

To this day, I am humbled and privileged to be an active part of Recovery Church. Even though I am on staff at Connect Church, I keep involved with our local Recovery Church and serve on the Board for Recovery Church Movement. I have learned so much about God and His Mighty Work. I have learned so much about myself and my own brokenness. I have seen the favor of God in unparalleled ways. I love the ministry of Recovery Church and I wouldn't miss being involved with it for the world. I can honestly say that I am a better Pastor, a better man, a better husband, and better follower of Christ because God has allowed me to rub shoulders with some of the most brilliantly broken people in the world who just so happen to love Jesus with all their hearts. To God be the Glory.

Max's Story
The Sober Pastor

My name is Max. I am a Christian, a pastor, and an alcoholic. I am sober today only by the grace of God and the fellowship of the program as contained in the recovery literature. I have been sober for over thirty years and have been in ministry for over twenty years (as of August 2022), much of which included working in some capacity with the addiction community. Currently, I oversee the Online Campus of Recovery Church.

Much of my experience of mixing recovery and church is filled with hope and promise; however, often, I was left with the feeling that something was just a little off. That neither the church nor the recovery program could be experienced in their unique fullness when combined. It was not until I met Pastor Phil and saw the vision for Recovery Church that I had finally found a home where my recovery and faith could not only co-exist and complement one another but truly thrive in their fullness.

At Recovery Church, there is a healthy tension between both church and recovery. There is a need for both in their fullness. We don't want to be so "churchy" that an addict or alcoholic doesn't recognize any elements of a 12-Step recovery meeting. Still, we don't want to be so "recovery" that there is nothing resembling a church service. Each area, both recovery and church have valuable elements and aspects to contribute to the addict and alcoholic who seeks sobriety. The church has the ability to teach true spirituality and give opportunities for worship that traditional recovery cannot provide, but the church usually is not equipped to get addicts and alcoholics long-term sobriety. In the same way, it may be a struggle for an alcoholic and addict to share in a church setting what they are experiencing or thinking as they travel on their sobriety journey. Imagine a church small group where someone shares about recovery-related items such as cravings, bed spins, being dope sick, or checking out the cameras every time you walk into a convenience store because of their previous intention of shoplifting. Sharing like this might not be accepted and most likely will not be understood or appreciated by those not in recovery.

In the same way, recovery meetings have the ability to help people get clean and sober and provide the needed support to maintain sobriety and are very open to spirituality but sometimes struggle with specific faiths or the mention of Jesus or the Bible. Recovery meetings are also not positioned to provide worship opportunities or Bible-based discipleship.

Recovery Church combines the best of both worlds. Someone during an open share at RC can quote the *Big Book*, the Bible, talk about Jesus, and throw in a swear word (although not encouraged), all within a three-minute share. In addition, an environment is provided for those who are still searching and trying to define their higher power, as the Christian faith and belief in Jesus are modeled.

One of the best ways to relay this reality is through the Bible story of Jesus appearing to His disciples after the Resurrection (John 20:19 – 31). Jesus visits the disciples in the upper room, and for some reason, Thomas is not there. Upon Thomas' return, the disciples tell him that they have seen the Lord. Thomas does not believe them, which on some level makes sense because this is an unbelievable claim. Thomas goes on to say that he will not believe "Unless I see the nail marks in his hands and put my finger where the nails were and put my hand into his side" (John 20:25). For this sentiment, he gets the unfortunate moniker of "Doubting Thomas."

Low and behold, a week later, Jesus again appears to the disciples, but this time Thomas was with them. Jesus goes right up to Thomas and says, "Put your finger here; see my hands. Reach out your hand and put it into my side. Stop doubting and believe" (John 20:27). Thomas recognizes Jesus and says to him,

"My Lord and My God" (John 20:28). Thomas had a conversion experience that transformed his life in a way that he would never waver again and led him to be a fruitful missionary and ultimately a martyr for the faith.

What is often missed or overlooked in this story is that the disciples allowed Thomas, in his doubt and unbelief, to stay with them for a week. They didn't kick him out or reprimand him. They gave him room and a place among them in the week in-between. When Jesus did reappear, Thomas had his "My Lord and My God" moment, but it was only because the disciples had given him the space to stay. Recovery Church is the week in-between. There are people in Recovery Church who have experienced the saving and transforming power of the resurrected Jesus, and there are people who have yet to have their own "My Lord and My God" moment but are given the space to explore and ultimately recognize Jesus as their higher power.

Personally, it took me two years in recovery before I found myself in the same room with Jesus. It took time. It was a process. Initially, I wasn't ready to believe. I needed the space to discover. I needed to see and to feel his nail-scarred hands before I could believe. But then I had my very own "My Lord and My God" moment. My life and my recovery have never been the same. This moment changed the trajectory of my life. Recovery Church creates the space and the opportunities so that we get to be present for others as they experience their own "My Lord and My God" moments as they experience the love, hope, forgiveness, and redemption that comes from experiencing a spiritual awakening through Jesus.

How it Works in The *Big Book* says, "Rarely have we seen a person fail who has thoroughly followed our path," and it is often said that Bill W., the founder of A.A., actually wanted it to say 'Never.' There is a path to sobriety – there is a way to stay clean that does not fail. In addition, the 12th Step promises a

"Spiritual Awakening" as 'the' result (in A.A.) or as 'a' result (in NA) of the steps. Interestingly, the 12th step doesn't promise long-term sobriety but a spiritual awakening. I would argue that it is not long-term sobriety that brings about a spiritual awakening but that a spiritual awakening is what brings about long-term sobriety.

Early in my recovery, I desired to be "spiritual," not "religious." I had been raised in church and always felt welcomed there but didn't experience or see any real-life change. I didn't have a problem with God or the church. In fact, I had a positive feeling toward both. I was concerned because of my drinking and drug use, as well as my constant lying and stealing, that I wouldn't be accepted or deserve God's love or blessings. Therefore, the spiritual approach seemed like a better option than the religious one. I would later discover there was much overlapping in those two approaches.

I always believed that God was love. I knew that I didn't earn or deserve God's love – I had no ill feelings toward God because of it, I knew I was a liar, a thief, a cheat, and an alcoholic, and if God was an umbrella of love, I just didn't fit under God's umbrella.

Then, shortly after sharing my 5th Step, I had a significant experience with God's love. I attended a college-age Bible study that introduced me to the man who would lead me to Christ (and later become the best man at my wedding). He taught me about Jesus' love, as well as his forgiveness.

There is a scene in the movie Good Will Hunting that helps to illustrate my experience. The main character, played by Matt Damon, is a genius from a rough neighborhood in Boston who struggles with anger issues and getting in trouble with the law. He meets with a counselor who is played by Robin Williams. In one scene, Robin Williams is reviewing the abuse that Matt Damon's character suffered at the hands of his foster parents. And Robin Williams had this exchange with Matt Damon where he repeated the same sentiment to varying reactions from Matt Damon:

Robin Williams: It's Not your fault...
Matt Damon: I know...
Robin Williams: It's not your fault...
Matt Damon: I know...
Robin Williams: It's not your fault...
Matt Damon: Annoyed and exasperated, "I know..."
Robin Williams: It's not your fault...
Matt Damon: You better not be lying to me...
Robin Williams: It's not your fault
Matt Damon falls into a Robin Williams' hug as he balls loudly.

This was similar to my experience with God and, more specifically, my experience with Jesus. Listened to this altered version of the same exchange.

"Max, Jesus Loves you..."
I know (I have heard that all my life... It's a nice sentiment, not sure it really applies to me, but nice nonetheless.)
"Max, Jesus Loves you..."
I know, that's a good message... (a message I have heard since I was a child attending summer Vacation Bible School)
"Max, Jesus Loves you..."
Annoyed and exasperated, "I know" (I've heard this message already – leave me alone – that's great for you, but doesn't really apply to me.)
"Max, Jesus Loves you..."
You better not be lying to me... ("I am going to let down my guard and trust you. You better not be misleading me because I cannot afford to be hurt again, and I feel very vulnerable at this moment.")
"Max, Jesus Loves you..."
I accepted and embraced the Love of Jesus and fell into his arms as I experienced a Spiritual awakening.

What rocked my world was the fact that Jesus did love me and that I did fit under God's umbrella of love after all. It didn't matter that I identified as an alcoholic, a liar, a thief, and a cheat, nor what was contained in my 4th Step Inventory or even my 8th Step Amends list. Jesus loved me for me, not because of what I did. This is the same truth that is often trumpeted at weekly Recovery Church meetings.

The message that Jesus loved even me, not only changed my life, but changed the trajectory of my life. My new purpose in life is to share a message of love and hope to others and help others experience the same life-altering experience that came from "making a decision to turn my life and will over to the care" of Jesus. Recovery Church is a perfect environment to experience this phenomenon, as well as share with others. This continues to be my life's purpose, whether in the rooms of recovery, speaking at a rehab, or giving a message at Recovery Church. God's love is for you, too!!

Another way I can share this powerful truth is through a parable from the Gospel of Luke. It is the third of three stories shared about lost items – the lost coin, the lost sheep, and the lost son that come from Luke 15. The parable of the lost coin shows God's great love for all his people and will not give up trying to bring every lost person to Him. The parable of the lost sheep is a favorite about how one sheep wandered off from the other 99 sheep, and the shepherd left the 99 to find the one. This shows how a sheep unknowingly wandered off, and the shepherd went to find him. So many of us identify as the sheep and are sometimes frustrated at the fact that no one came looking for us. That is because many of us identify as a lost sheep (someone who accidentally wandered off) when we are more likely the lost son or daughter that intentionally left home.

The parable of the lost son tells a story of someone who doesn't feel like he quite fits in. It tells of how a younger son demands his inheritance from his father, takes it, and goes off and engages in "riotous" living – most alcoholics and addicts can certainly relate to riotous living and would describe their own lives in similar terms.

The lost son ran out of money, friends, and opportunities as famine hit the land, and he is forced to take a job feeding the pigs – not a suitable place for a good kosher Jewish boy. He realized that even the servants at his father's house were better off than himself, so he left and headed on the long journey home. As he got closer to home, his father saw him "a long way off" – indicating both that the father was looking for the lost son to return home and that he recognized him from a far off – his shape, his gait, he knew his son and was filled with compassion and love for his child. So much so that he ran to his son – not the usual action of a wealthy Jewish man. He embraced and kissed his son, and the son tried to spit out some lame apology that he had been practicing the entire way home. Instead, his father quieted him and instead called his servants to prepare a big party with the best fixings to celebrate his son, whom the father said, "For this my son was dead, and is alive again; he was lost, and is found.' And they began to celebrate" (Luke 15:24).

This is a story of recovery. This is a story of faith. This is my story of recovery and faith. I realized I was in a pigpen, and I too shuffled back to the father with my pathetic excuses, and I was told by the father, "I LOVE YOU!!" That was a message I needed to hear…This may be the message you need to hear: YOU ARE LOVED – despite it all… and sobriety is like when the Father throws this underserved party…robes, rings, fatten calf – talk about a party!! Once we get sober: The party has been going on ever since!!

George's Story
The Boy Who Dreamed of Flying

As a kid I had a big dream! I wanted to be an Apache Helicopter pilot. One of my favorite shows growing up was Airwolf! Man, Stringfellow Hawke was the coolest guy ever! Though The Airwolf Helicopter was not an Apache, it spawned my thrill for flight! I wanted to fly high, fast, and dangerously. Little did I know that my dreams of flying high would come in a more destructive way. No one ever dreams of growing up to be an addict.

I was born into what should have been a normal 80s family. Yet, one of my earliest memories is of my mom having me and my two siblings in the car, bags packed, and backing out of the driveway as my dad waved goodbye saying he would join us soon. Divorce struck our home. The day of my father rejoining us was not to be and my search for a father figure began.

Moving to Florida, my mother did the best she could raising three rowdy kids while working the graveyard shift at the local hospital. Her long nights away from the home left us with plenty of time for "experiments." I remember taking my first drink in the fifth grade, one of my mom's beers from the fridge. I justified it, even then, by thinking beer wasn't bad because my mom drank it. I was also in D.A.R.E. and knew drugs were bad, but beer?

On the last day of school for my fifth-grade year I came home ready to start my summer. I walked into my home a happy kid moving into middle school. My house was empty, but I heard some laughter coming from the back porch. I walked out to find my older sister and her friends smoking something that smelled funny. How do you keep the little brother from snitching? Give him a hit. In a single year, around the tender age of 11 my whole world changed... and not for the better.

In the years to come my story is the same as any other addict; if you could drink it, smoke it, chew it, pop it, sniff it, drop it then I was doing it. That is, all but shooting. I am scared to death of needles, or at least I was until it was the only way I could get high. One night, faced with an ultimatum to either shoot or not get high, I overcame my worst fear in order to feed my addiction.

At my worst I was 120 pounds soaking wet and smelled like I just crawled out of a dumpster. My "friends" came up with a name for me that I didn't know they called me until I got clean, Junkie George. In my early 20s I met my drug of choice that would ultimately take everything from me, Meth. I was on the run from both criminals and cops alike. I was quickly running out of places to go. I remember going to my mother's home and finding the doors locked. I knocked. She answered and said, "I will feed you, I will let you shower, I will let you get some clean clothes, but you cannot stay." On that day I knew things were at the worst. Yet, I kept going.

Shortly after, I had a divine intervention with the Sherriff's Office. My arrest would lead to my imprisonment in the State of Florida. It was here that I surrendered to Christ as my Lord. You see, I had known Him as my Savior since about 13 years old. My friend's mother took us on a vacation. While driving down the road she would look to the backseat at me asking me to pray some prayer to let Jesus into my heart. I remember thinking "Lady, I will pray whatever you want me to, just watch the road!" That day Jesus became my Savior, I accepted His payment for my sin, but it wasn't until I got to prison at twenty-three that I knew I could no longer run my life and I allowed Him to become my Lord. A huge gap between Salvation and surrender.

I got out of prison with the best of intentions on living a new life of sobriety and faith. Yet that was not to be, at least not right away. I went back to my hometown and found my mom at a bar. I walked in and without a second thought I ordered a drink. That drink led to more drinks then to a night club. I kept telling myself that I was acting like a "good Christian." I wasn't fighting, I wasn't cursing, I wasn't doing drugs. I was "okay." By the end of the night, I ended up at an after party in a bathroom with two "friends." Out came the cocaine. I remember thinking I shouldn't; but as it got passed to me, I got ready to use. Just at that moment a real friend walked in the door and said, "George! What are you doing?" I turned to her and said, "What? I can do just one." As those words rolled off my lips, I knew I was in grave danger. I put the drugs down and asked my friend to take me home.

The next day, broken and defeated, I knew what I had to do. I picked up the phone and called my sister, who by this time had gotten her life together and was sober and recovering through a 12-step program of Alcoholics Anonymous (used with her permission). She introduced me to a program of recovery that would help provide me with the tools to live a life of recovery beyond anything I had ever heard before. My first two years were some of the most promising years in my life. I thought I would stay sober forever. Sadly, that was not to be.

Along with my recovery, I began to peruse a ministerial calling. I began to experience the uncomfortable friction in the rooms of recovery when I would mention the name of Jesus. I would be asked from time to time to "tone it down on the religious stuff." I couldn't understand how people didn't see the God I knew and loved all over the pages of the *Big Book*. I also began to meet many great mentors and teachers in the Christian faith. Many of these men did not understand addiction recovery at all. A few asked me things like "do you really need 12-steps? Can you really not have just one drink?" Or they would say things like, "All you need is Jesus, not those steps." I mean, who can argue with "all you need is Jesus!" There seemed to be such a large divide between the Christian faith and program of recovery I had come to know. So, after two years working the steps, I left the rooms of A.A. with a chip on my shoulder. In very short order I relapsed.

How could this be? Didn't I have enough faith? How come my other Christian friends could have one or two drinks and not end up in a crack house after they empty their bank accounts or sell their possessions? I had to do something. Around this time someone had told me a church was doing a "Christian 12-Step" program. I went over and checked it out. Amazed! Here was a program utilizing almost the exact same steps while freely and openly talking about Jesus! I felt right at home. Many grateful years of recovery followed as I threw myself into the Christian 12-Step program.

Yet, something was always off. I remember taking training to be a leader at this Christian 12-Step group and being instructed that we could only use their materials. No other books, specifically the *Big Book*, or other recovery materials were to even be mentioned. Nor were any other 12-Step groups that were not affiliated with the Christian 12-Step group I was attending. I remember inviting my friends from the rooms of A.A. and it never really going well. The Christian 12-Step group had too many rules for them, was way too "structured" and a little too "in your face" for someone who wasn't really sure what they believed yet. Some of those friends stuck around, many did not. I remember feelings of grief knowing that we could do better for our recovery community as the body of Christ. I thought the one place a person should feel accepted as they are, should be a "Christian Recovery Group." But for many years I would just go along with the status quo of "Christians helping Christians" in recovery while my grief and burden for my fellows in recovery and the divide between the church and groups like A.A. grew in me and around me.

In 2016 I began working for a treatment center. We had a new Executive Director join the team and one of my fellow co-workers, Wayne, said he wanted to take me to this guy's Recovery Church. I pushed it off for a while, knowing my disheartenment with how I perceived Christians doing recovery. Finally, I gave in

and went with my friend. This single experience would spark something in me that would change me forever!

My friend Wayne and I walked into Recovery Church of Lake Worth, and I was blown away! In the middle of downtown, up a flight of stairs, and into a bar we walked. Only this was no bar like I had ever been in before. Sure, there was guitars and memorabilia on the wall, and it had a cool name, The Bamboo Room, but this was something else entirely. We walked into a room of 250+ addicts and alcoholics and they were worshiping God! I saw tattoos, tank tops, colored hair, and short shorts. I saw well-dressed men and woman sitting side by side with people that looked like they were in their first day of detox. When I looked around, I saw "Junkie George" in every seat that was filled with someone struggling to stay sober.

Up to the podium came the new Executive Director of the treatment center I worked for and Founder of Recovery Church Phil Dvorak. I remember him interchangeably going back and forth from scripture and the *Big Book* like a well flowing river. I remember him connecting the beliefs of the Christian faith found in the Bible and the ideas of recovery found in the *Big Book* in such a way that made more sense than anything I had ever heard before. As the night closed and we were getting ready to depart, Phil came over to say goodbye. Probably like some little fanboy with glitz in his eyes, I said to Phil, "You have to come do this in Vero Beach!" What felt like a gut punch, he said "No"… only to follow up with "but we will help you do it." And with that, the journey of Recovery Church Vero Beach, the first campus plant from the Lake Worth RC, was born.

I fell in love with Recovery Church because I experienced,

for the first time, the middle ground where people from the rooms could find Christ and Christ could be sent out to people in the rooms. Recovery Church spoke both languages, Faith and Recovery. It was like the two disconnected links in me finally

connected and things began to make sense for a young pastor in recovery.

Recovery Church Vero Beach, Florida had its small beginnings out west of town in an outlet mall plaza. Wayne, Michelle, Ken, and I worked with Phil to bring Recovery Church to our little community. Sure, we didn't start downtown in a cool named old bar with 250+, but that wasn't the point. We had to find out how to do Recovery Church in our environment. As God led, we followed. Now Recovery Church Vero Beach is meeting downtown, across from our courthouse, next to our Substance Abuse Coalition, and we are seeing an average of fifty addicts and alcoholics new and old in recovery coming every Wednesday night! All because God led us to give away what He had given to us… OUR RECOVERY!

I share this story with you because learning to fly didn't happen like I thought it would. No, I never became a helicopter pilot, but I did learn to go high, fast, and dangerous. Like many addicts and alcoholics, the wake of pain and destruction rippled into the lives of those closest to me. I have lost more friends to drug related deaths than I can count on both hands and feet. I don't know why God pulled me out of the darkness other than to take what the enemy meant for evil and allow Him to use it for good. I share my recovery openly and honestly with anyone and everyone who will listen because it's not me who got me sober, but it is God who granted me the serenity to accept the things I could not change, the courage to change the things I could, and the wisdom to know the difference. If He can do it for us, He can do it for you or for your loved one!

"When we became alcoholics, crushed by a self-imposed crisis we could not postpone or evade, we had to fearlessly face the proposition that either God is everything or else He is nothing. God either is, or He isn't. What was our choice to be?" (Alcoholics Anonymous World Services, p. 53)

"In reference to your former manner of life, you lay aside the old self, which is being corrupted in accordance with the lusts of deceit, and that you be renewed in the spirit of your mind, and put on the new self, which in the likeness of God has been created in righteousness and holiness of the truth." Ephesians 4:22-24

Bridget's Story
The Catholic Christian

My name is Bridget, and I am a Catholic Christian and recovering alcoholic. I'm also a mom, a wife, a daughter, a sister, a friend, a coach, and an entrepreneur. If you're reading these pages right now, I want to encourage you that you're in the right place, and there's a plan and a purpose for your life that is bigger than you can imagine, and it starts with a simple belief that you were meant to be here right now, at this moment to receive this story. You see, my story is about direction, decisions, and destinations. When I first started drinking at thirteen, I felt amazing, I felt relieved, I felt like time stopped, and I could just enjoy not feeling my feelings. But the truth is that time waits for no man. While I was drinking, time continued to take the precious minutes of my life away from me that I freely gave. Well, I continued to drink and do things I wouldn't otherwise do sober; the desires that I used to have to get married, have children, take trips abroad, and ambitions for a career slowly began to fade away and feel far from me.

I felt like God loved me only when I was being good, and when I was moving away from Him, that He didn't love me at all. Therefore, I started to feel uncomfortable around others, around God, and things of religion and faith. But the truth was, I treated alcohol like my god. I would run to alcohol when I was afraid, I would run to alcohol when I was lonely, and I would run to alcohol when I wanted to feel comfort. Instead, today, I turn to God for those things, but at the time when alcohol was my God, there was nothing else that mattered, and for you reading this right now, the verse that comes to me is, "God, help my unbelief." When I don't believe that you can help me, I believe, help my unbelief. In Mark 9:24, a man seeking the Lord's help came to Jesus and fell to his knees weeping and said, "I believe, help my unbelief." Because the truth, regardless of whether I believe it or not, is John 3:16, "For God so loved the world that He gave His only son, that whoever believes in him will have eternal life." Like John Maxwell's quote, "Not, however, but whoever believes in him...". No, there's no *but* in there, it's whoever believes in Him, not, however, if they don't do this, however, if they don't do that, *whoever* believes in him will have eternal life.

After finally becoming so miserable in my thinking and seeing that my drinking was taking over my life, I couldn't differentiate true from the false anymore. I realized that God was pursuing me. I got into a relationship with a man who was getting sober, and I would sit in meetings with him and say that I was just there to support him. This is proof that God pursues us and sometimes uses defects to get our attention. I was only sober so that I could compete with this man's recovery because the truth is, I thought he was going to leave me, and I was leaning into insecurity, which is why I would sit in those rooms in those meetings with alcoholics in recovery. I didn't just wake up one day and say, "I'm ready to be sober." God pursued me just like He pursues all of us, and sometimes God gives you the window of opportunity, which is really a door that is easy to walk through, and that's what this relationship was, though I did care deeply about this man. My desire to be in recovery grew stronger, and I got a sponsor, which drastically changed my life. Jeremiah 29:11, "'For I know the plans I have for you,' declares the Lord, 'plans to prosper you and not to harm you, plans to give you hope and a future.'"

That summer, we were sitting in the rooms for six months, and I heard God in my heart say, "I can't use you for my plan and my purpose when you're drinking." I then started to work the Steps and I began to experience the transformation everyone spoke about. Being in A.A. was like having glasses for my blind eyes and a hearing aid for my deaf ears. The new relief was that I stopped thinking about what others thought about me. I went to A.A. for my drinking, but I stayed for my thinking. Before recovery and gaining an active relationship with

Jesus, I was always thinking about what others were thinking about me. After the drinking problem came the people problem. Many of us are like this - this is the definition of egotistical with an inferiority complex. I always like to remind my sponsees and friends of this simple and humorous way to remember that it's crazy to try to think about what other people are thinking. I call that the definition of insanity! The truth is when you're feeling out of your mind, you are probably in somebody else's, and when you're in somebody else's, you're definitely out of your mind.

The solutions in the 12-steps helped me with my thinking once the drinking was out of the picture and this is what helped me stay in recovery. I had come to realize that drinking was just a symptom of the mental illness of alcoholism I had experienced. What happened next was the promises came true, and I got married and began having a family. Shortly after, I found Recovery Church Movement and started leading worship. The Big Book says, "I was quick to see where religious people were right and made use of what they offer." I started to understand in Scripture when Jesus said, "Come and follow me." It wasn't a request, it was a command out of love, and Jesus was commanding the ones he loved to preach the Gospel, heal in his name, carry their crosses, and walk alongside other people, especially in the recovery world. I left my old beliefs and my old life at the door. I left my hesitations, fears, and limiting beliefs. I turned my will in my life to the care of God as I understood Him every day and continued to enlarge my spiritual life. I have three boys and they witness me singing at Recovery Church often and sometimes are on stage with me while I hold the microphone. But the truth is, once I got sober, it didn't mean that life on life's terms always got better.

Satan is totally cool with me showing up as a Christian or tempting me into my old life. I've read the book, "The Screwtape Letters," and in one of the letters from Screwtape, who is a wise demon, he says, "Your person has become a

Christian." Satan replies, "That's fine. Help them to always be distracted and notice all these other things around him that are annoyances to him. Help him to notice when he's at church that the choir is just a little bit off key. Help him to notice how the woman in front of him has started to fall asleep and snore quietly. Help keep him from realizing that the enemy is truly present." In this book, the enemy that Screwtape is describing is God. The more I entered into being sober-minded and enlarging my spiritual life, the more I was aware of the spiritual battle. Satan was fine with me being a Christian, and now his 24-hour job was to help me to become uninspired to share the message of the 12-steps and the Gospel. My advice to you is don't let him stop you. Sometimes in recovery, I've learned that I have to do what I don't want to do, and I do not get what I always want. Today, because my desires are filtered through God's desires, through Scriptural truth, and spiritual mentorship, I will go to church whether I feel like it or not. I will go to a meeting whether I feel like it or not, because sometimes feelings aren't your friends. Your feelings can lie to you.

I ask myself often, "Am I showing up in my life as a spiritual being having a human experience, or am I showing up as a human being having a spiritual experience?" The difference is that being a spiritual being, having a human experience, means that everything functions in God's economy. I see my life, my marriage, my relationship with my boys and other people, and my career as spiritual, and God is my employer. I used to be the one who was the human being having a spiritual experience, before I got into recovery, and before I knew that God wanted to be a part of my life. He has given me a romance with life. I used to take God out of the box when I wanted him with my foxhole prayers, and then I would put him back in the box when I wanted to go drink, be in relationships, or do my life the way I wanted. Do you have the God in the box mentality? It's good to ask yourself that question. Today, everything is filtered through my relationship with Christ: my life relationships, money, and business choices. These choices reflect that I am a Christian, sober woman. Prayer, Scripture, and faith-filled relationships are the support system of my life, and I believe, know, and trust that Christ is my provider. Today, because of sobriety, I have a loving husband, three boys, and three dogs. My life is very similar to the 21st-century Brady Bunch.

I have a career that allows me to be mission-focused with my priorities and values. When I continue to keep doing the next right thing, what I know to be true, and practice my partnership with God, I will stay sober one more day. I will be able to serve others for one more day with the gifts that God has blessed me with. Whenever I'm feeling far away from God, all I have to do is get on my knees. "The spirit is willing, but the flesh is weak," as it says in Matthew 26:41. I will get on my knees and ask God to give me the next right thought or action. All I must do is ask God to help my unbelief, to show me and to make me the woman He wants me to be today, not the woman I think I should be. Not the woman that I want to be, but the woman that God wants me to be today. I go to Proverbs 3:5-6, "Trust in the Lord with all your heart, lean not on your own understanding; in all your ways acknowledge Him, and He will make straight your path."

I want you to know. If you're reading this book, Recovery Church Movement has changed my life. It has become the most God-driven ministry that I've been a part of. At this time, I have been sober for sixteen years. I want to encourage you that God has a plan and a purpose for your life, and He is going to give you the power to show up every day to be sober and sober-minded so that you can serve people and help others start to have a romance with their own life. God can get you well too. I'm truly grateful to Pastor Phil for listening to God and following God's plan for his life. Without him listening and taking the window of opportunity to start Recovery Church Movement, none of us might be where we're at today.

And I encourage you to sharpen your listening skills because there's a big plan for you. God qualifies. "God does not call the

qualified, He qualifies the called," and you have a calling on your life just like I do, and the first step is to be sober.

Chrispy's Story
The Militant Atheist

Hi! My name is Chrispy (first name Chris, last initial P. Just say it fast). Today I am a grateful recovering addict and a believer in Jesus Christ. That is not, however, how my story starts. One of the first memories I have from childhood is being sexually molested by a stranger. This set me on a path of playing the victim. As I got older, I began to get molested by people that went to church on Sunday.

I began to suspect that God wasn't real. I became really withdrawn and had difficulty talking to people. I was raised in a household where alcohol and drugs were not allowed. I didn't have any real interaction with them in my childhood. I got married the summer out of high school. I think I was trying to make the family life I didn't feel I had growing up. I was just plodding along, mostly doing whatever my wife told me I should be doing. It wasn't until her twenty first birthday (I was twenty-one and four months old) that I had my first drink. Man, that was the ticket. Suddenly, I could talk to people. People wanted me around. I was the life of the party. Quickly the alcohol progressed to weed. That was enough for a minute. Then my world fell apart. My marriage imploded and I was once again lost and alone. It was the first time my daughter helped save my life. I wanted the pain to end. I had my little Geo Metro up to 90 (about max speed) and had a telephone pole picked out. The image of my daughter standing over my grave, not knowing why I had done it, stopped me from going through with it.

I did the next best thing and started doing meth. That drug was the first chemical I became dependent on. After a few years, I "quit" doing meth but continued to drink and smoke. I started experimenting with anything that would take me out of myself. The list of drugs I have taken is long. It would be easier to list the ones I have not tried. I will spare you that time. The point is I was trying everything to avoid facing myself. I met my second wife, and the using spiraled. We were the perfect couple. We believed the best amount of drugs was "all of the drugs." I began to use opiates heavily. The town I lived in had a "pill mill" that prescribed lethal doses of opiates. They were always around. After some time, the pill mill was shut down, and most people I knew started doing heroin. Not sure why I didn't follow in their footsteps; early God intervention is the likely answer. I did, however, make a conscious decision to stick to alcohol for the most part. The drinking took a while. It is slow and insidious. You have the illusion of control until well after it has control over you. I hit the bottom of my physical and spiritual limits. I was trying to find a place where I could go to treatment locally. At the time, I was living in Washington State. I was fed up with trying to find somewhere. I went to take a nap and asked my wife to help me find a place. When I woke up from that nap, she handed me a piece of paper with one phone number.

I called the number, and the guy ran my insurance, called me back, and said, "I think this is going to be a great place for you. I will make the flight arrangements." My response is heavily edited for your sake and any future readers of this story. Think drunken sailor mixed with heavy object dropped on your toe, and you will surmise the gist. "Flight arrangements?! Where are you?" He told me he was in South Florida. Now at this point, I doubled down on the drunken sailor. This guy wanted me to go as far away on the continental United States as I possibly could get, from my wife and kid, to do treatment. After I calmed down, he assured me that he had gone through the program, and it had helped him a lot. I got on the plane thinking I was going for a few days and going back to my old life, sober and fixed (even I find my naivety cute sometimes).

God sure did have a different plan for me. While I was in treatment, my wife told me she wanted a divorce, was moving on with another guy and then disappeared with my son. I am not going to lie; I thought the worst thing that could have happened to me had. I will tell anyone now that it was the best thing that ever happened to me. It forced me to stay in Florida and face the real problem, Me. I actually would tell everyone who would listen that two things were not going to happen. 1) I was NOT coming to God. 2) I was NOT staying in Florida. Four years sober, I still live in Florida. At the beginning of this story, I already told you in whom my faith lies. It's all about Jesus. I think back to all those times I made those two statements. I imagine God chuckling to Himself.

Back to the story of what happened. So, I am sitting in a treatment center, trying not to lose my stuff. They packed me into a "druggie buggy" (the vans they used to transport us to meetings) and took me to this place called Recovery Church. I was livid. It was in a bar called the Bamboo Room and they were talking about Jesus. I knew this would happen. I claimed to be a militant atheist. I had spent most of my adult life using biological and scientific reasoning to prove that God didn't exist. The reality was I kind of suspected God did exist. I just couldn't understand how He could have let that stuff happen to me when I was a child. I had started reading the *Big Book* of A.A. There was all this talk of a spiritual solution and a whole lot of talk about God. I still really didn't want to have anything to do with God. I was, however, finally desperate enough to try anything. I started working the 12-steps. While I was doing that, I heard the same spiritual message coming from Recovery Church. I kept going to RC. I would tell them I didn't believe what they believed, and I didn't even want to touch a Christian with a ten-foot pole. I just felt more spiritual when I was around them. RC did the best thing, the ONLY thing, that would work with someone like me. They didn't pressure me. They just let me have the time to get to know God.

Now God was working double time in the background. At 90 days sober, I had posted my 90-day cross, chip, and tag on social media. My cousin told my daughter about it. Now, I hadn't spoken to this girl for the last six years. In the meantime, she had found God, which was a sufficient excuse for me to be done with her. It is pretty funny looking back at how I saw the world. She was the one to have an excuse not to have anything to do with me. She was the first person to actually model what Jesus had modeled for all of us. Squishy (her nickname) had no reason to forgive me. When I was in her life, I caused nothing but chaos, but more often than not, I wasn't in her life. She didn't want anything to do with me. She reached out anyway. She knew what I know now. If I want to live in forgiveness, I have to forgive.

Squishy came back into my life when I needed her the most. She became my little spiritual adviser. To be honest, she has been a better parent to me than I ever was to her. She was the first person to tell me that the voice I was hearing, telling me to go back to what I was doing, was not just my addiction talking to me. It was the enemy. Satan wants me back in my addiction. When I was "in my cups," I was one of the enemies' best agents. Not only was I as far from God as I could possibly be, but I also helped pull everyone around me further from God with all of my chaos. Squishy let me know as I walked toward God, the enemy would come at me hard. When my faith was young, the enemy knew it was his best chance to break me.

Around this time, I had started going to a meeting every Monday night. It was a spin-off of Recovery Church. It was a Christ-centered 12-step meeting. It used the Life Recovery Bible and the *Big Book* of A.A. This was where I met Roadkill Rob. How he got that name is one of my favorite God stories. It is his story to tell. I had begun to realize that I needed a sponsor who had beliefs more in line with mine. God will put the people you need in your life, not the people you want. Roadkill Rob is an old-school Italian male. He is a *Big Book* thumping, Jesus-loving, hardcore 12-step sponsor. In other words, not a pushover. When God put it on my heart I needed to ask him to be my sponsor, my initial reaction was "Noooooooooooo! Anyone else God? I mean, like anyone." Rob was what I needed. He put me through the 12-steps as prescribed in the *Big Book* of A.A. The 12-steps did what they were designed to do. They closed all the doors that the enemy used to attack me. They put accountability in my life. They set up a daily way of life that continually points me toward God and keeps me from slipping into my old habits. They made me face what my real problem is, me. No one in the world needs to change. I need to change. The reality is I can't change. I can only stop fighting God. He is the one that can change me. Everything previous led to what happened. I finally met God in my heart. I had a spiritual awakening, a psychological change.

How is it now? I don't think I am equipped to do this part justice. I will tell you this...I now have purpose in my life. My conversion wasn't quite the road to Damascus, but it was close. The one place God put me was the one place where there was a Recovery Church. I have been able to watch what God can do. From just one RC to RCs all over the country. I have been able to play a part in growing God's kingdom. I take other men through the steps regularly. I get the great honor of watching the light come on in men that were so lost there was no return. Alcoholics and addicts have a special relationship with God.

When you come to God forced to your knees by the weight of death, you know what you have been saved from. Alcoholics and addicts are the people that Jesus came for. I believe that we are the group of people that have been equipped to bring revitalization to the church. I have finally come to a place where I trust that God loves me as much as He does. That is true freedom. All the sexual, physical, and mental abuse. All the years of hurting myself and others. It was what had to happen. Now God has taken all of it. He has taken my pain, suffering, and anger and it is now a gift. It is a tool that I get to use to reach others. Men don't want to talk about sexual abuse. I can reach them where, otherwise, they would not trust me. I would not change a second of my past if I could. Everything that happened led to me meeting God. I told God there were many things I wasn't going to do. Thankfully He just does what He does anyway. I believe that purpose is the key. He is using me to spread His story. Get a sponsor, work the steps, and help others find God's purpose for their life.

Maribeth's Story
The Pastor's Kid

I guess you could say I don't have the typical "addict story." I grew up in church as a pastor's daughter. My childhood really was just about perfect. I had amazing parents, a loving sister, and a life surrounded by constant reminders of God's love and mercy. At nineteen years old, my dad suddenly passed away, and it flipped my whole world upside down. I was angry. I felt betrayed! I started using and drinking. Slowly at first. Then I gradually found myself feeling so miserable being sober that I had to use drugs and alcohol to cope with my everyday living. Fast forward thirteen years later. At this point, I completely ruined my first marriage, my friendships, my job, my everything.

In 2018, I started dating a wonderful man, who is now my husband. My husband was a recovered addict. Soon after we got together, we became pregnant with our daughter. This meant no more drugs and no more alcohol. I felt so confident that I could go without, and I did. I stopped using and drinking completely, but I became even crazier. Sudden emotional breakdowns, always crying, lonely, depressed. I finally had everything I wanted. A beautiful baby girl that I'd prayed for my whole life, my two stepdaughters who were my entire world, and a husband who unconditionally loved me and would do absolutely anything for me. But I was still going insane. Finally, my husband asked me to go to an A.A. meeting with him to "see what he does." Little did I know this was the first step to my intervention.

This group opened so many doors in my life. It introduced us to Recovery Church. For the first time in my life, I realized I had a problem. I knew all the "right answers," but I had no relationship with God. I was such a hypocrite. After digging deep and finding my real "Goliaths," I learned for once in my life I can be me. I could be the woman God desired me to be because I found my identity in Jesus Christ. My identity no longer bound to who my parents are or a social status. After fully surrendering myself over to God and taking the steps to make the decision to change my life, I no longer feel miserable. I can control my emotions. I have learned I am GOD's daughter. Nothing I have done in my past or will do in my future will change the way God feels about me. The transforming grace He has so graciously given me is unbelievable. I am so thankful God was faithful, even when I was not.

Cindy's Story
The Cancer Survivor

My love affair with addiction began with a trip to a bar on my twenty-first birthday, for no other reason except I thought it was the thing to do. You turn twenty-one and you're supposed to drink, right? It moved from two trips to the bar every few weeks to drinking at home every weekend. Every month or two, my husband and I went out for a night of drinking at our favorite bar. After my son was born, I realized I couldn't drink out in the open as much as I wanted. So, I kept a lot of it secret. Our refrigerator was always stocked with some wine, which I enjoyed a glass or two of after my son was asleep.

When surgery for my cancer caused me significant pain, I was prescribed Percocet and it quickly became part of my daily regimen. When I ran out and the doctor cut off my refills, I found out who was selling pain pills and began buying them on the street.

In 2018, I was diagnosed with cancer for the second time. This bout was more intense and painful than my first, so I killed the pain with wine, marijuana, and pain pills. I was a great actress through it all, making people see me as a strong cancer warrior in public and hiding behind a mask of drugs and alcohol at home.

In May of 2019, I was approached by a pastor I never met before. It must have been God speaking through him because he saw my addiction without me mentioning anything except that I was looking for a church to start attending. He gave my name and number to Tina Dunham and she introduced me to Recovery Church in Richmond, Indiana. In July 2019, I admitted I had an addiction and I needed help breaking its hold on my life.

Now I'm two and a half years sober. Was it hard? Yes. Do I

still struggle? You bet. What keeps me from taking a drink or hitting a joint? It's the people I've met in my recovery journey who have cheered me on to victory, the laughter of my grandchildren when they see their grandma smile and wrap them in a hug, and the God who has been with me through everything. Recovery is the best decision I have made and I don't want to go back to the person I used to be.

Kentucky Dave's Story
The Probation Officer

My name is David, and I am from Georgetown, Kentucky. I was born with a severe birth defect in both my legs, which resulted in a total of about eight surgeries. Growing up, my parents tried to make every attempt to make me feel as normal as possible. I was raised by two loving parents and grandparents in a middle-class neighborhood. My father worked at a bank and my mother at a dentist's office and school cafeteria. I was raised in the Nazarene Church, where we attended every Sunday. I regularly attended Sunday school and was involved in the youth group.

I grew up believing that I was saved on Sunday and was going to heaven and then would "backslide" on Monday and was going to Hell. This was very difficult and caused a great deal of anxiety in my youth. While in the eighth grade, I suffered a bleeding ulcer. I tried drinking from ages sixteen to seventeen, and when I went to the altar at church, I gave my life to Christ. At this point, I was a senior in high school and had a christian case of the "Don't." As long as I don't sin, everything will be ok, and I will get into heaven.

In 1983 I graduated High School and was off to college. Everyone was drinking except me. I remember it just like it was yesterday. My friend Dano beat me in a game of pool and began to laugh and taunt me. A family curse was an explosive temper, and here is where it showed up in spades. All my childhood being different and laughed at due to having a birth defect showed up right here. I couldn't stand the humiliation any longer and got a bottle of Kentucky Bourbon. I knew from church that I had fallen from the love and approval of God. I just couldn't live this perfect life any longer.

I began drinking and quit going to church. Alcohol allowed me to be the person that I saw others attracted to at parties.

Graduating high school, I had never had sex, and since I was going to Hell anyway, I thought, "if ya can't beat em, join em." I soon had a nickname "Tanner" and began to create this character that nothing was beyond the scope of what I would do to get attention. I was kicked out of college, let back in, and barely graduated with a minimum GPA in Community Sports Recreation.

Following college, I married my college sweetheart and was hired as a Recreation Director of a Prison. During this time, my son was born and we bought a house in my hometown. In 1994 I applied for and was hired as a Probation and Parole Officer in a small town next to my hometown. This was the first time I saw this thing called addiction, and I didn't know what I was really seeing. In this small town, I saw the effect it had on the community, friends, family, and the individual. I couldn't understand what was going on and why these people couldn't quit. Why they kept going back to something that was killing them. I wanted to help these people and did the best I could, but I didn't really understand what was going on.

On March 2, 1997, there was a severe flood in the town of Cynthiana, Kentucky, where my home office was. On this date, I was unable to get to the office due to the high waters and went to visit with a friend. He asked me if I wanted to take a pain pill. I didn't take drugs; I just drank alcohol. The person asking me to take this pill was someone I looked up to in high school. He had the fastest car in the parking lot and dated the most beautiful woman I had ever seen. I asked him what it would do to me, to which he responded, "I don't know. I have never taken one, I'm sober, but if it does anything bad to you, I'll take you to the hospital." To this, I said, "ok." It was the most incredible feeling of my entire life. For the first time in my life, I didn't feel unlovable, less than, or inferior to anyone. I asked him how much it cost, and he said $5. I knew there were seven days in a week, and 7 x $5 was $35, and I could afford that. I was going to feel like this for the rest of my life.

Fast forward a few years, I now had a daughter, and I was taking not 5mg a day but 200mg a day just to not be dope sick. This thing that had made me a better person, dad, and husband was now destroying my life. I no longer had a decision to use or not use; I had no choice but to use. I now understood what those people on my caseload when I was a Parole Officer talked about when they said they "started off doing drugs, and then the drugs did them." I was getting high so I could coach my kids or just so I could go to work, which was now working on a horse farm because I could no longer hold a professional job down. My marriage was fast falling apart, my relationships were fast falling apart, and I blamed my birth defect for everything.

On Monday, November 11, 2013, I received a call from the Sheriff's Department and they wanted to talk to me. It was a charge of me taking a ring from a dear friend and pawning it. My wife texted and said, "I don't want you home when I get there," followed by a call from my father, who said, "Son, you better come down here with your mom and me. It sounds like you have a lot of trouble." I initially thought I would pack a gym bag and stay with mom and dad until things blew over. Well, things didn't blow over; they blew up. I was living with mom and dad; I had a criminal case in one court, a divorce case in another court, and a soon-to-be ex-wife calling wanting things done yesterday so she could get divorced, sell the house, and move on with her life. I was juggling dope sickness, two lawyers, two courts, and the only person who would talk to me was the person who introduced me to pills and my dope man. I had no answers for anything, and as a former Probation Officer I was heading into the Probation Office, where I once trained officers on the use of firearms, force, and pepper spray, as a client who was now going before the court on misdemeanor charges of Receiving Stolen Property Under $500. I was sentenced to two years of probation and three weekends in jail. I was on probation, living with my parents, and had only one friend left. I was all alone for Thanksgiving, Christmas, birthdays, and Father's Day came and went with not even a text. I watched the lives of others on social media while my life got even worse.

After the divorce, I would travel an hour and forty-five minutes one way to get my pills from my old dealer. I was the worst addict ever to live, only knowing one person who sold the pills I had to have. I was offered a job as an exterminator, which I took. This quickly resulted in me going into the house and looking through medicine cabinets to find my pills. I don't know if it was paranoia, my conscience, or the Holy Spirit, but my actions were eating me alive. I was in a mental state that was so bad that to this very day, I can't describe the feelings of depression and self-hate. I met a guy while serving weekends, whom I got with on social media, who said he had a place in Florida I could go for treatment. On November 14, 2018, I hopped on a plane to South Florida where I entered a treatment facility with a faith-based program. Pastor Dan was the pastor of the program. When I first met him, I figured he was like all the rest and would tell me I was going to Hell for all the bad I had done. This I had already figured out on my own, so I didn't need him to tell me. I just wanted some relief from the pain of being an addict. Here the foundation was laid for a true understanding of who God really is and who I really am. I was introduced to a local church and service work. I found a Christian sponsor who took me through the steps. I moved into a halfway house and worked on the setup team at the church. During this time, I met a great man of God, Pastor Mitch. He encouraged me to take online Bible courses and to attend and get plugged in at the church. He mentored me, and I was able to see the love, grace, and mercy he told me God had for me. I was able to see it firsthand through a man of God.

One night a friend of mine asked me to go see his girlfriend sing at something he called Recovery Church. As soon as I walked in, I knew there was something different about this place. People began to tell their stories, and then I heard they were pastors. I couldn't believe God took someone who was addicted to drugs, had been to jail, and was now preaching and helping others. This church that claimed to be "a church for addicts by addicts" was a church for sinners by sinners, and I had found a group of people who were as messed up as I was and who were sober and happy. Something I did not think was possible. I knew I was going to attend this church every Thursday night. During this time, Pastor Dan got me into a minister's course. During the course, we were asked what our two-to-five-year plan was. I said I didn't know, but I felt like it had something to do with this Recovery Church. Several weeks later, Pastor Mitch said that our church was going to start a Recovery Church. I truly felt like I had a direction and purpose for the first time in fifty years.

On June 22, 2022, our church launched Recovery Church Delray. It was during the COVID pandemic, so we were not sure if we were even going to have our first service. Well, the first service went off without a hitch, and I was working shoulder to shoulder with Pastor Mitch setting up, tearing down, and encouraging others as I was encouraged. I had finally found a place that was home to me, where I knew my identity and my purpose in life. I finally found what I was created for and who I was in Christ. I began by telling my testimony and was then asked to preach. I had preached a sermon at a Christian treatment center, but this just felt different to me. Today I encourage others through being a manager of a halfway house, a mentor to young men at the church through service work and being able to sponsor these men through the Word and take them through the steps. I have seen men come in broken and no relationships with children and family like I did. I see them now picking up one-year crosses and getting custody and visitation rights back with their children. I see people come in who tell me they are only here because their treatment center brought them here, only to see them just a few weeks later give their life to Christ and get baptized. I have been asked to baptize people who came through the same treatment program I did. I can't believe God took a crippled drug addict like me and used me to introduce these people to the Savior of the World.

I have so many blessings today that I could never put them all on paper. But as I am writing this, I am preparing to leave my house in thirty minutes to fly home to stay with my parents for the weekend. I will spend time with my daughter; we will go shopping, go to the county park lake, where we will eat donuts (yes, right after we get out of the gym), drink milk, and talk. Then before we leave, we will feed the ducks donut holes and name all the ducks. My daughter is twenty-three and still wants and needs a daddy. I will visit my son, who is now a Police Officer in Lexington, Kentucky. We talk about dealing with people as it relates to law enforcement, trucks, guns, and my biggest deal in my life, his daughter and my first granddaughter, LUCY JEAN!!!!!!!! YES, I AM A G-POP!!!!!!!!

Today I understand who I am in Christ. This is HUGE because, as an addict, I never knew who I was or whose I was. I also have a purpose as I help young men be sons to parents and dads to their children. I am scheduled to graduate from Bible College in August 2022 and am currently working on becoming a board member representing Recovery Church on the Palm Beach County Chaplains Board. My parents are both eighty-two, and my father tells me several times a week he is proud of me. This is something I have longed to hear my entire life.

I just want to say I understand Recovery Church did not give me eternal Salvation or wipe away all my sins as no one or any organization can ever do. What Recovery Church did for me was create an environment by bringing people together where I, first of all, felt welcomed and not judged. This allowed me to not worry what someone was thinking or saying about me so I could receive the true word of God. It also allowed for all the opportunities for fellowship, service, and learning without judgement. This allowed God the opportunity to deliver the promises that He is who He says He is and that He will do what He says He will do. I can't imagine my walk with Christ today without Recovery Church and the opportunities to serve God and others.

Worship Mike's Story
The Orphan Who Found His Father

As I look back over my life, I realize if there were a recipe to make an alcoholic or an addict from trauma, my early years included all the ingredients. I do not, however, blame anything that happened to me for what I became. Through hard work, prayer, and service to my Father and my fellow brothers and sisters, I recognize it is all part of a journey which ultimately led me to where I am today.

I was born in Manassas, Virginia, to a mother I do not remember ever knowing. The most that I can tell you about my parents is my mother was Caucasian and my father was African American. My earliest memories as a child are traumatic. I remember being in a foster home in Riviera Beach, Florida. I remember exactly where it is and can take you there right now. The foster parents who ran the house were very old. I remember needing constant attention, which didn't sit well with them. If I did not fall asleep, I was punished by being placed in a closet. I remember being afraid and lonely. I created little friends to keep me company. I would talk to them in that closet and get in trouble. The foster parents would turn the lights off to further reprimand me for talking while in punishment. That was the first time I was willing to go to any length to escape. I was lonely and afraid and didn't care how long I had to stay in the closet. I would have rather been in there all night with my imaginary friends than be alone for a few minutes.

While at the same foster home, I used to go to one of their brother's houses whenever they went to the dog park. One of my favorite people was there, whom I called my cousin. After several visits, while "Dunc" was asleep on his recliner in the

59

living room, I played in the other room with my big cousin, who was around thirteen. I was not yet three years old. I remember him demanding I perform sexual acts I didn't fully understand. I remember saying that I did not want to. I remember being punched in the face and told if I cried loud enough to wake up "Unc," he would kill me. I remember complying and being more afraid than I ever had in my entire life. I hoped no one would ever find out what had happened. I didn't understand why he would want to do that and wondered why I was so helpless. Luckily, I was adopted not too long after by a hard-working middle-class family. They were nice, and things were really good in the beginning. As hard times came, the dark secrets of their past started to infiltrate the facade they had created, much like we all do to escape. He became abusive, and she began to have mental breakdowns. I was afraid of him, and there was often evidence of beatings on my face and body. He battled alcoholism and crack addiction. Eventually, I moved out of the house, or should I say, ran away. I was ultimately arrested and placed back into foster care.

My first foster house was more of the same. My foster brother was the biological son of these foster parents and was a large individual. He was 6'3" and was being recruited by the best D1 colleges to play strong safety or outside linebacker. He was not always mean but often would beat me up for things like defeating him in video games. It happened a lot because I was really good and very stubborn.

One day I realized things were never going to change for me. My birth mother had given up on me. My "favorite cousin" had sexually abused me. My adopted father had physically abused me and then given me up. Now, here I was, alone, being beaten up by my "brother" and mom. At a turning point in my life, I was being beaten up, again, in front of his cousins. I fought back with everything I had. I swung and swung until I realized he was going down. I tried to run and grab a weapon to keep him down, but I was not fast enough. As he grabbed me and threw me down, his cousins stopped him and said, "We respect that you fought back. We will not let him hit you anymore." That was music to my ears. I was not afraid, and I was respected. At that moment, I realized I was willing to go to any length to escape the feeling of being afraid and helpless. I was willing to go to any length to be accepted and respected.

For the next few years, my life became a constant cycle of going to new foster homes, getting in trouble, going to jail, to another foster home, and repeat. I ended up in a youth development center known as "Chobee," a level eight youth facility for juvenile delinquents. During that time, I developed the persona of the man I wanted to be, hiding the reality of who I really was. Fighting became the norm for me, and I started to bury myself in a bunch of lies. I created a false bravado to hide my insecurities. When I got out of the facility, I remember my detention officer was unwilling to send me back to my old neighborhood. Instead of returning to any of those homes, they put me in a group home while I awaited an opening in Boca Raton. I got the opportunity, and it was the best and worst of both worlds. Boca was a place where I was able to experience life among people. We lived very different from the life I was accustomed to. There was a different culture and a sense of entitlement I was not used to. Also, I realized I could make several different types of friends. Being the chameleon I was, I took full advantage of the different groups. My favorite groups were the jocks and the stoners. I liked the jocks because of how they drank and the stoners for another manifestation of the same reason. This is where my addictive nature began to take off. I was always able to make friends with anyone doing any drug.

After I graduated and lost the outlet of sports to help me slow down my drinking and drugging, things really started to escalate quickly. I was a person who cocaine dealers liked to have around. They were always doing lines and sharing. There were times I would be awake for days. One night I washed my face in the sink and blood shot out of my nose. I liked getting high, but it was destroying my nasal passage, so I started looking for a "better" way to use it. Someone suggested I try smoking it, and the rest is history.

Crack cocaine was my new master and controlled everything about my life for about a year. After realizing how badly I was hooked, I told God if I had to live the rest of my life like this, I would rather die, but if He could deliver me from this addiction, I promised I would serve Him.

The very next day, I was in a ministry which helped the homeless, drug dealers and addicts. I stayed there and remained sober for eighteen years, including nights and weekends. The power of God was evident to me there. I knew He was a great God and powerful King. However, I didn't really get to know Him as a loving Father and gracious Lord. I was pursuing a "checklist" type of salvation instead of just being loved by God. After a while, I lost hope in a battle I seemed destined to lose. I tried and failed, was condemned, and withdrew time after time until I no longer felt worthy of God's love. After my first failed marriage, I was lonely and trapped in the life of a lustful single man repeating those steps of trying, failing, falling into condemnation, and withdrawing. After a while, I was at such a low point I was willing to settle for anyone who accepted me as I was; and just in time, I met my second wife. She was twenty-one, had a car and an apartment, and she wanted me. She was the one. The only problem was she smoked weed, but I could deal with that...or so I thought.

Eventually, I began drinking and smoking weed. I held down a job until I found out there was a problem at home. She had slept with several different men, and shortly after that, I was in jail with a domestic violence charge on my record. God sent His angel in the form of a childhood friend who bonded me out and took me to his house in Plantation. I tried to be sober there with some help from AA, but could not get out of my head. My drinking got worse. I started blacking out and decided I would use cocaine to prevent that. I lost everything, including my desire to eat, bathe, or even live. I eventually ended up in jail, and not a moment too soon. In jail, I participated in the prayer group but refused to lead. When I got out of jail after about ten months, I promised I would not repeat my mistakes. As soon as I got some money in my pocket, I was off to the races. I thank God when I ran out of money, I heard Him tell me this run would lead me to death. I reached out to that childhood friend again, but this time he told me the ONLY way he would help was if I went to rehab.

I had no choice, so I conceded, and it was the best thing that ever happened to me. February 3rd, 2020, is my sober date. I struggled through the pandemic with only videos of my favorite preacher and a desire to do more. As soon as the restrictions lifted, a friend of mine invited me to Recovery Church. This is where God reminded me of Matthew 5:6, "Truly blessed are those who hunger and thirst for righteousness, for they shall be filled." I was hungry for more, and I know Recovery Church is where He sent me to be filled. I found people who love the Steps and love Jesus. Recovery Church is a fellowship of like-minded individuals who walk with me, love me and love on me. I have been able to serve coffee, serve as a Worship Leader, and as a minister. I truly thank God for Recovery Church Movement and their part in helping rewrite my story for His Glory!

Laughing-Bear's Story
The Loner

My name is Laughing-Bear. I am a grateful alcoholic from Alaska and a follower of Yeshua the Messiah, "Jesus." Most just call me L-B, a name that my Pastor and dear brother, Max, gave me.

My family history. Mum, a daughter of a mafia hitman, was an alcoholic who supposedly owned a perfume factory in Columbia. Dad would fit into the bad guy's role in the movie "Deliverance." Both tried to escape their families and get a fresh start at college. Mum sought the Highest Power; Dad became a stereotypical reservation drunk. Most Indians should not drink! He embraced the dark side. Thankfully he ran off with another woman when I was in the 8th grade. When he drank, he told me it was Cow Pee or Moose Pee. I was embarrassed as a young child and told no one my dad drank pee. I grew up "Reservation Poor" and became a loner, always feeling like a "Pork Chop at a Kosher Wedding" as resentments built.

My first drink was in sixth grade with my dad in a bar in Montana. I blacked out! I didn't often, as a teenager, touch the "Fire Water," but the handful of times I did, I was out of hand but still standing.

On 22 December 1984, my world blew up with a roar that I still feel to this day, changing my life forever! I ended up with P.T.S.D. (Post-Traumatic Stress Disorder), a nighttime movie complete with sound effects and the smells of death replayed in my mind. I became fearful of sleeping. I would drink to numb myself to get brave enough to try sleeping. Often when awakened by nightmares, I grabbed the bottle to knock myself out. I had no use for anything but hard liquor. Drinking was not a social event; I drank alone. I wrote this poem titled "1984" to express what I went through.

1984

Twenty-two December, nineteen eighty-four,
The day my world blew up with a deafening roar.

We were both alive, called the other friend;
Never had a clue how this day would end.

I was driving north, you were driving south,
Never would have dreamed... blood gushing from your mouth.

Heavy fog was freezing, roads were beyond slick,
Your car slid into my lane, crushed you like a brick.

Struggling up the bank, making it to your car,
After peering in…. wished I'd stayed afar.

Could hear you were gurgling, struggling for each breath;
Wrapping you in my coat, marching towards certain death.

My mind then snapped! I began to scream;
A picture etched in memory, repeatedly saw in dream.

Your funeral massive, sat in back row;
Preacher began to speak, God, he did not know.

He spoke lies, words that didn't fit;
'God couldn't always watch our back.' Inside I screamed... bullshit!

'Sometimes the devil grabs us, taking us far away,
Much to God's shock and to His dismay.'

Walking from our church, never did go back;
Finally sought relief, poured from a paper sack.

With screaming, I'd awake, your crushed face I would see;
I'd pour another drink. Rest, it eluded me.

A haunted man, until my thirty-ninth year;
Family now gone, shedding of more tear.

Finally, met a Friend, who gave me peace within;
Put down the bottle, serenity did begin.

Now live in solicitude, my family's my dogs;
But I can laugh again, and sleep like a log.

Kevin, you're still missed, healing tears I don't lack;
But I can go through anything, I've been to hell and back.

I cried out to Adonai, "God," seeking help, but the dreams worsened. I believed in the Messiah of the New Testament, and at the age of eleven, on 15 November 1974, I had, with my Mum's guidance, invited Him into my life. But in truth, I had more of a head knowledge than a heart experience.

Later on, when my wife practiced infidelity, rather than deal with it, I just buried the pain with the jug. While on active duty in the Air Force, she ran off with my best friend and took our daughter. I drank harder. I reached out to the hand of A.A. in 1988. While still active-duty military, a Full Bird Colonel psychiatrist told me I must never look inside; it would be unhealthy and dangerous; no way was I going to do a 4th-Step, so I was in and out of A.A., trying to see how I fit in. I saw only the differences, not noticing the common problem. That is when 'WE' take the first drink, and we lose the power of choice. My job was the 'Enlisted Club' manager where we had our bar, which only made matters worse. I worked from 3-11 pm, Monday to Friday, so I had weekends to drink every night after getting off duty. During this time, I had little to do with the church after what had transpired at the funeral with Kevin. Believing that most at church didn't really care for alcoholics, I kept low on the radar.

After medical retirement in 1989 from the Air Force, I returned and embraced A.A. I finally heard other Vets with P.T.S.D. and could relate to them and their nightmares. Like many of them, when I drank, my body would awake the next day in spots: spots like Las Vegas, Puerto Rico, the neighbor's wife's bed, you know.... spots. Because I was fearful the Full Bird Colonel knew what he was talking about, I was sticking to his instructions and refused to look deep because I felt the 4th Step was just too dangerous.

I married a wealthy man's daughter, the trophy wife of my

unrealistic dreams. We had three children. I became a professional land surveyor with a nice home, golf course, country club, toys, Scout leader, and community-related programs. My family at times attended a local church, but I always felt less than and knew not to let others know I was an alcoholic because I feared my family would be shunned, although I had put down the bottle and white-knuckled it.

Her father hated me as he ruled his empire, and I was polite but would not bend to his control. Finally, I had enough and told Him that I was going to outlive him and would come pee all over his grave someday. Yep! We went to hyper-hate, and he disowned his daughter. So, when we divorced years later, he was more than willing to help her remove me from her life. While doing the 9th Step, I sent a letter making amends for the grave incident, which was totally out of line for me to ever state such an ugly comment.

Though I had put down the bottle, there was one big problem: there had never been any change on the inside! I was both emotionally and spiritually dead. I had quit A.A. I didn't need it; I was doing well in the eyes of the world. I was a "dry drunk," also known as being on an "emotional hangover" and on an all-out "emotional jag." Though a good husband and father, I was not there. A funeral or Christmas brought the same dead feelings, and it was impossible to cry! And... oh yes, those nightmares were still there to greet me.

At the height of my blind success, in 2001, another big event took place that rocked my world. Feeling like a "Stud Duck strutting around at a Texas rodeo" while working on the road as a land surveyor, I was taken out by a man who was drunk and driving backwards down the road. I never saw him coming. No longer able to work, the trophy wife left and found a guy who had more money and emotions. I was in physical pain, still dealing with P.T.S.D., the old resentments, and now had new emotional pain and resentments. Picking up the jug again, I was off to the races, and within about a week, I was back to the point of consumption of years before.

Desperate and calling out to God one night, I was listening to the rock band 'Creed'; I heard the song "One Last Breath." I realized I, too, was six-foot from the edge. I know now this was the first of what I call the fingerprints of God! In divorce court, I learned for the first time I had supposably been a Navy Seal Sniper, had worked as a Professional Mercenary, had a court-ordered vasectomy since I had fathered so many illegitimate children around the world while working as a mercenary, had even been the President of the Spokane Chapter of the Hell's Angels. That's the untrue rumor I am the proudest of! I had been the owner of a Yamaha back in the day when I rode motorcycles. I must have been one tough biker to ride it as a Hell's Angel. I could not afford a lawyer, and because I was getting slammed, I just kept my mouth shut. Mum told me that I must not say anything, even if true, that could cause harm and pain to my kids. I refused to use the facts I had that would have been helpful but hurtful! I allowed myself to be slaughtered. The resentments grew.

Seeking a fresh start, I decided as soon as I was capable, I'd prepare for a move to Alaska since my children were not going to be in my life because "I was just too dangerous." But I realized I had to get help, or I would not live long enough to hunt moose, pan for gold, fish for salmon, or enjoy the Northern Lights. I decided after I saw the fingerprints from the Highest Power that it was time to seek outside help for P.T.S.D. and other things. I did this for six months, and when I knew I was in a good place with my P.T.S.D., I returned and embraced A.A. once again, as suggested by my counselor. I was a desperate man desiring LIFE! I was going to strive for sobriety like it was starting to rain, and I was the 3rd of three monkeys in line to get on Noah's Ark, and if you know the story, only the first two got on. I was determined to get on at all costs.

My close friend, Irv, took me under his wings and became my Sponsor. I set it up so that my counselor and my Sponsor could freely talk to each other, and I was not to know what was communicated between them. Irv, on Tuesday nights, ran a faith-based recovery Bible Study. I was all in and started to find a shift from just head knowledge to a heart experience: the two finally connected. I was at a meeting where for the first time, I found believers in Jesus who loved me and wanted me around as they also battled the bottle. I finally felt like I belonged. I also started attending closed A.A. meetings. I kept coming to those meetings because I loved the laughter, as they were not a glum lot, and I desired to have all the Step promises.

Directing me to dive deeper into the *Big Book* of Alcoholics Anonymous, Irv had me read chapter 14, page 544, "Freedom from Bondage," and chapter 15, page 553, "To Handle Sobriety," right at the get-go. He explained that holding onto resentments and self-pity brought on festering mental attitudes. It does not rob the other person of their energy, only mine. It does not mess up their dreams, only mine. It does not steal their happiness, only mine! And, if I forgave them as Jesus would require, all the resentments would fall away. When you have resentments, it is like looking through a "FORK," you're in jail; the ones you are looking at are not! My prayer for my children's mother was, at the time, the best I could muster, and I did it only because I did not want to drink again. I would not repeat those first prayers as I have to realize that profanity is NOT a sign of spiritual growth, and there are ladies that will be reading this. I no longer use such words, as Adonai, and the Twelve Steps have removed such from my life. But as I kept praying over several days, I realized my prayer had changed, and I was genuinely praying heartfelt blessings.

I soon found a relationship with the Great Mystery, the Indescribable Three-in-One. It was the first time my head knowledge and my heart linked up together with this Highest Power. I also fell in love with the Biggest Book as well as the *Big Book*. I worked all the Steps the best I could with Irv, stayed in counseling, and learned I had to use the 3 R's when dealing with someone that was rubbing me like a rhino porcupine. Retreat,

Re-think, Re-act! In addition, I was to embrace "The Four Absolutes" that Dr. Bob used and loved: "Absolute Honesty, Absolute Unselfishness, Absolute Love, and Absolute Purity." They were to be my yardstick.

With the blessing of my Sponsor and counselor and with six months and one day of sobriety, I rolled into Fairbanks, Alaska! They told me if I kept working the 12-Steps, the principles for each Step would take place and grow. And "one day the 'you' you were supposed to be will meet the 'you' you are now! Arriving in Alaska late at night on 9 September 2002, I moved into a little cabin.

The next day I went shopping with some of my grubstake money and saw the Fingerprints of the Great Mystery. The first person I met was a Legendary Musher. This stranger stopped me and started asking all kinds of questions. He realized I wore braces on my knees. He had bad knees as well! For some reason, I opened up to Him and even told him I had six months and two days sober time after I put down the bottle on the 7th of March 2002, so I counted the 8th of March as my start date. Now I know he gave up the bottle years ago, but he never claimed to be involved in A.A. But he told me I would be at the men's A.A. meeting every Friday night, and if I was not there, he would know, and we would have a problem. For some reason, I said, "Yes sir," and though nobody ever told me what to do, he did, and it saved my life. Later, I found out he was a musher, and he convinced me to mush my own dog team. I, to this day, wear a yellow Anorak (an Eskimo coat) like he did when mushing.

Even though I jumped into A.A. in that part of Alaska, I no longer had a church family. I was blessed to be able to attend A.A. meetings seven days a week because the majority of Alaska does not have meetings. In fact, there have been places I have been that, in order to drive to a meeting, if the roads were plowed, was 140 miles in each direction. I still, in some respects, felt spiritually separated since I did not have a group of drunks to pray with who read the Biggest Book. But there were more fingerprints from God. A World War II Veteran at a co-ed A.A. meeting named Judy ordered me to sit down beside her and became my "grandmother sponsor." She loved Jesus! And my co-Sponsor, Mike M., did as well. I started doing service work, and Judy told me the what, when, and where of this service work. In A.A., I found love, help, true friendship, and acceptance. It says in the Biggest Book in Psalm 68:6a, "God settles the solitary in a home." I found a home but wanted a church family.

I relocated to the part of Alaska where I now live to go to college to become a drug, alcohol, and domestic violence counselor. Because I wanted to work with drunks, I tried to put some clues out there that would be noticed by a person with a drinking problem. I acquired custom license plates - one reads, "IMSOBR." For my other rig, I got a plate that read "STEP 1" to not only draw drunks to me but to remind me I am powerless over people, places, and things. This was a helpful tool over the years, but there was a negative ramification I had not counted on. I tried to find a church to attend, and at two different churches, when they saw my plates, I was told, "We do not like drunks; please do not come back." There were a couple more, but when they realized I was in A.A., they would not even bother to shake my hand. So hurt, I just did not look anymore for a church body; I guess you could say I threw the baby out with the bathwater because I just did not want to feel that pain again. But, as my first Sponsor had taught me, Irv, not to build resentments, I prayed for them. I dove deeper into reading the Biggest Book and prayer while having a daily quiet time with the Great Mystery and going to A.A. meetings, although at times, I lived where these meetings were not always available.

Many of the hardest things I have faced took place while embracing sobriety, as well as many wonderful blessings beyond my wildest dreams. I became the musher of a dog team and have become the musher they think I am. It says in the Biggest Book that a kind man is good to his animals. That has to come from the inside; it cannot be faked because they will know. I built a cabin and live off-grid; hunt, fish, pan for gold, mush under the Northern Lights, became a published writer, oil painter, and learned to play the Native Cedar Flute. I went North and started to work for a mushing tour guide since I had top-notch dogs, and due to the working of the 12-Steps, I had become a better people person. By this time, all twelve of the 9th Step promises had taken place in my life, with the last of those promises taking place years before after three years, two months, and seven days of working the program of Alcoholics Anonymous. "Fear of people and economic insecurity will leave us."

But one of the hardest things that happened while there was receiving my fifth TBI (Traumatic Brain Injury), and all these injuries were on the same spot on my head. I lost for a long time the ability to drive, had to learn to speak again, and I lost a lot of long-term as well as some short-term memory, but even in this, I saw the fingerprints of God. The Biggest Book and the *Big Book* did not slip from memory! I also ended up with what is known as Photosensitive Epilepsy. In short, flashing lights, fluorescent lights, computer screens, T.V.'s, and even smartphones could put me into a seizure. Suddenly, I could no longer attend A.A. meetings since so many had their *Big Book* on their smartphone, or the meeting room lights were fluorescent. I became trapped, avoiding society because even cash registers could set me off. Also, a couple of times when visiting a church, I had to sit outside away from everybody as the screens in the front of the church used for songs and Bible verses would set me off to seizure land. I had to isolate, so I was turned on and dove into A.A. phone meetings.

One of the problems I face where I now live is there is not always phone service, and it can be a little spotty depending on weather and solar storms. But I was usually able for several years to get in at least a couple of meetings with an old flip cell phone that gave me some connection. Many in Alaska have come to healthy sobriety by working with others just over the phone.

Because I had found success with maintaining my "emotional sobriety" and "emotional stability" with phone A.A. meetings and was honored to chair some of them, when I heard there was something new called "Zoom" meetings that had just taken off in a big way since Covid had shut down most face-to-face meeting, I was interested. Then I heard it was over a computer and my heart sank. I could not use a computer due to my seizure problem, and there was no internet in my part of the world. I could not even have a phone landline. But a friend said you could call in and do it over a flip phone when you have a signal. My heart was warmed with joy and hope.

I went to the meeting that I had been recommended, and I was hooked. I found a new A.A. family. I attended as often as I had signal, and Adonai blessed me with a long string of being able to phone in, more fingerprints of God! I was told by one of the members, Max Ingram, that there was a Zoom meeting called R.C. (Recovery Church). It was a church for people like me who did not fit well in a stereotypical church and felt they could not bring up their faith in an A.A. meeting. The Recovery Church is like a bridge between the church and A.A. I had found, I was sure, the answer to many years of prayer, a church that would accept me and where I could be of service as well.

Also, a dream I had been praying about for a long time was to be able to have a recovery Bible Study once more with others who did not feel able to share at a church or a 12-Step meeting. Our prayer team was small, but we diligently prayed. I reached out to the organization responsible for the Life Recovery Bible, sharing with them my desire, never imagining it would be over a Recovery Church online meeting. I was given their blessing.

So, I dove into my Recovery Church Online meeting and found a home, my church family. I decided after God put it on my heart to approach Pastor Max about the idea of a Life Recovery Bible Study under the umbrella of Recovery Church. I sent him all the details I had, and since he is my Pastor, I told him I would submit to his authority and only do as he directed. He came back with a resounding, "Let's do it." So, with a few modifications from him, we launched a Thursday Recovery Bible Study. With a paper format in hand, because I could not see over my flip phone, our weekly Bible Study took off. Wow! The fingerprints of our God were all over this. And when I thought it could not get any better, I was hit with a new round of fingerprints that I am still in awe over today.

I received a call from some people living down in the lower 49. Yep, Alaska is over Hawaii. They felt led to supply me with a computer that had a special screen that worked well for most with Photosensitive Epilepsy. And to make things even better, a company was located that, with their satellite system, I could have the internet and a phone landline. Wow, all of a sudden, after years, I could send an e-mail, research some of my hobbies, and the best part - I could now see the voices I had so wondered about since March of 2020. I was blessed, and the best part was being able to go to church three days a week at Recovery Church Online.

One of the greatest gifts that came to me with the online Recovery Church was being able to partake in virtual communion. Before joining my new family, I had only been able to have communion twice since coming to Alaska. It still brings tears to my eyes when Pastor Max leads us in this extremely holy event. Though I started partaking in the sacraments when I had just a phone connection, it became even more powerful to this alcoholic by being able to see the Bread broken and Cup lifted before my eyes. Though I deeply appreciate every sermon as well as every share, virtual communion is the biggest gift R.C. Online has brought to this

Alaskan.

Our Bible Study on Thursdays, such a highlight in my life, is still growing. I have a prayer team that prays for me as I seek our weekly topics. Two of our members were on the original prayer team asking Adonai for months to provide a Bible Study for us, and this was before they joined Recovery Church or even online meetings. At the end of Thursday meetings, we have a prayer request time we all take to heart. It says in Proverbs 27:10, "As in water face reflects face, so the heart of man reflects the man." Oh, we so see this reflection in Pastor Max and those who are now embracing Recovery Church.

I would never have dreamed when I started this trudge twenty years ago, that I would find anything more inspiring than mushing a dog team under Northern Lights, watching the sunset over mountains that reach to the heavens, or listening to wolves singing to the moon, BUT.... then... God gifted me with Recovery Church. It became this Bush Rats' biggest highlight. I am humbled and in awe of God's goodness!!! May my journey bless you. Know you're loved 5 much, that is 3 more than 2 much. Just me, L-B.

Grace's Story
The Single Mom

I am a recovered drug addict and alcoholic, saved only by the grace of God and transformed into a new creation thanks to Jesus, the 12-steps of Alcoholics Anonymous, and the fellowship with the body of Christ. I grew up in the suburbs in a nice home where everything appeared normal and I honestly thought it was normal, until I later found out that my "normal" was not everybody's normal. Well, in A.A., it seems to be a lot more "normal," or shall I say common. Since I could remember, my dad was an alcoholic and was very verbally abusive toward my mom and me. I felt like I was always standing up for everybody, including myself, at a very young age. I found myself not feeling good enough, not worthy, not important, but I couldn't figure out why. In hindsight, I know I had a God-sized hole inside of me from day one.

By the time I was fourteen, I was hanging out with all the wrong people and doing all the wrong things. I felt like I could finally be myself, and I was accepted, but it also included a lot of alcohol and drugs. Within six months, the crew I was hanging around with had already sat me down and told me I needed to stop drinking because my behavior was out of control. I think I laughed it off and was drunk the next day. Shortly after, I started doing coke and smoking crack and from there, my life went downhill really quickly. I was extremely rebellious and could not be controlled. I knew in my heart what I was doing was not ok, but I didn't have any desire to stop.

When I found heroin, I would say that's when things really got bad; but honestly, they had been bad from the beginning. The enemy had me by the throat the moment I started drinking. I was a slave to sin, and drugs were my master. I would do anything to get that next one, and I was riddled with guilt and shame. Over a five-year span, I was in and out of fifteen treatment centers and countless intensive outpatient, homeless, couch hopping and burning every bridge in my life. I became unrecognizable, and no one wanted to be around me. I had very literally pushed every person in my life as far away from me as possible. The enemy had me right where he wanted me, isolated, hopeless, completely out of my mind, and not desiring change. BUT GOD. God had different plans.

It was probably around June 28 or 29th. I had just overdosed and my sponsor had come to try to find me and get me out of there, but I chose to not go with her and stay in literal hell killing myself. That is insanity and the power of drugs and the devil. Those things are powerful, but God is greater. He stepped in and changed my entire life. I woke up the next morning, and I believe The Lord gave me a desire to change. The first honest desire to change I think I ever had in my life. I realized I didn't have to live like this anymore and that there was hope, so I picked up the phone and made a call, and I went back down to Florida and started on this incredible journey I definitely don't deserve. But that is the grace of God, isn't it? I've been sober since July 2, 2013, and I pray I stay the course one day at a time and follow the Lord for all the days of my life.

When I arrived in Florida, I went to detox and then straight into a halfway house. I had no conception of a higher power, but through working the 12-steps, I came to believe in one. The Lord is so gracious that one of the rehabs I had been in brought us to Calvary Chapel in Boca Raton, and I was led by the spirit to go back there in early sobriety. The worship music spoke to my spirit and really drew me in. To this day, it is all I listen to, and it has a special place in my heart. Worship music has saved me on many days. It reminds me of the truth of who God is. The Word tells us in Isaiah 61, where there is a spirit of heaviness put on a garment of praise. So, when I'm going through the battle, I praise through it until I'm on the other side. I will tell you the first couple of years of my sobriety, I was definitely not a sanctified version of myself. I was very rough around the edges and still living in sin, but again the Lord is patient and gentle and so good to me. He has slowly but surely transformed me from the inside out and made me a new creation and continues to refine me daily.

Around two years sober, I found out I was pregnant. I was in love and we were excited and everything was great. Our son was born on March 23, 2016. He is the greatest gift I have ever received other than salvation and sobriety. My fiancé did relapse, and he died on March 19, 2017. Once again, because of the grace of God, I had had a solid enough foundation in the program that I knew exactly what to do when life as I knew it was falling apart. Reach out to others, seek God, don't stop praying, keep going to meetings and keep showing up.

Over eighteen months, I had become severely anxious. I had panic attacks all day long. I felt completely trapped by circumstances. I was so plagued by fear and depression while trying to keep my head above water. On top of that, I was taking care of my baby, my business, my program, and myself. It was so, so, hard. I had a handful of years sober, and I truly wanted to die some days because the pain was so great inside of me, and it didn't matter how much I prayed or talked about it or wrote about it. It just wouldn't leave me. It was grief, and I didn't have the time or support to be grieving.

I had been going to church all these years, but I was never really involved. Well, I guess one day, I had ears to hear, and I joined a small group, and that is where the Lord really started ministering to me and changing me. I was in a group with solid believers who started speaking truth into my life. Everything started to change, slowly but surely. I got a hunger for the Word like never before, and I started reading the Bible every day. I had questions, so I asked them. I didn't understand a lot of things, so I called my friends and discussed them, and I studied the Word. The Lord softened me, pulled out the bad weeds, and replaced them with good seeds. His truth really does set you free. I joined the prayer team and really got myself plugged in with a great community of believers who hear and do the Word. I now lead others into freedom because we can only keep what we have by giving it away.

Life has not been easy, and not every day is fun and exciting, but I do have one thing that I never had. I've got the joy of the Lord. He is my strength, my portion, my protector, my father, my shepherd. When things are not going well, He is the place I run to for strength and shelter. When things are going great, He is the one I give all the praise and glory. I have now been going to Recovery Church Delray for about ten months. One thing I know for sure is God is on the move. We need Jesus with the 12-steps. Jesus is the way, the truth, and the life. I am so grateful for a place that bridges the gap. So many lives are being transformed by this movement, and I'm so grateful to be a part of it. Thank you, Jesus, for setting me free. Thank you, Jesus, for the abundant life you have given me. Thank you that you are growing me and changing me every single day so that I can look more like you. I am so grateful to be used by you, Lord. Do with me as you will, all for your glory.

Pam's Story
The 60's Radical

I was born in Oklahoma City in the 1950s and grew up in an irreligious family with no spiritual foundation. I was totally unprepared for the chaos that came with the 60s and the Vietnam War Era. During that time, I was in college, and by my senior year, I was carrying around Saul Alinsky's book, *Rules for Radicals,* chanting "Speak truth to power!" with no concept of what truth or power even were. I was a rebel without a clue!

As was common in the 60's, I began to drink and drug. However, unlike most of my friends, I did not "outgrow" the habit. Over the course of time, my use increased. In 1986 I moved to Florida, running from my addiction and a ten-year marriage that included all forms of abuse and violence.

In Florida, I found my way into 12-Step recovery and developed a "God of my understanding." That was better; however, at around five years of sobriety, I began to realize that, as the *Big Book* of Alcoholics Anonymous stated, my addiction was "but a symptom of my problem." By the end of my third marriage, I accepted that codependency was controlling my life, and my God was not big enough for a life I did not understand.

A.A. had taught me that the solution for all my problems was spiritual. While I was not interested in becoming a Christian, I was desperate and willing. I began seeking God with my whole heart. One Sunday, I attended church services at a local Christian treatment program with some friends, and it was there God kept His Jerimiah 29 promise. When I sought Him with my whole heart, I found Him. I received Christ's offer of salvation in 1991.

After a couple of years, my pastor said, "Pam, you know too much to be seduced by the ugly demons. Now you're going to be seduced by the good-looking ones." Truer words were never spoken. Over the next ten years, the Lord blessed me with a husband, home, children, a master's degree, a clinical license and professional career, a leadership position in the church, and I fell right back into the performance trap that had held me all my life. As the *Big Book* describes, I was once again "a victim of the delusion that I could wrestle satisfaction and happiness out of the world if I only managed it well." I had simply swapped the secular world for the church world.

What I learned was as long as there is one more thing you do not have, that you believe will fill the empty place in your heart, you have hope. But when you have everything you ever wanted and are still empty, you are, of all people, most hopeless. I have seen it often over the years. When we come to that point, there are four options: 1. to harden our hearts (and frequently pick up a hidden sin to take the edge off), 2. totally blow up everything and try to start over, 3. commit suicide or, perhaps the most frightening of all, 4. get radically serious about developing a personal relationship with God.

Since I had already tried the first three, I chose number four. As with any relationship, it has been a long and rocky road. I have considered walking away many times, but as was Simon Peter's response when Jesus asked him if he was going to walk away too, I have had to respond, "But where would I go?" When you have tried everything you know and are willing to try, there is nowhere left to go. Only Jesus has the words of eternal life (John 6:67-68).

May we all come to the place of Psalms 107: 31-32, where we "Lift up our hands and give thanks to God for his marvelous kindness and for his miracles of mercy for those he loves! Let's exalt him on high and lift up our praises in public; let all the people and leaders of the nation know how great and wonderful is Yahweh our God!"

Michael's Story
The Boy Next Door

Have you ever felt that you were in over your head? That no matter what you tried to do, you could not get out? Have you ever felt so hopeless that you thought you would never amount to anything and this was how you would be forever? Have you ever felt so alone you knew you didn't fit in even when you were in a crowded room? This was how I felt every single day for ten years during my active addiction. This is how my story became a part of His Story.

I grew up in a small suburb just outside of Chicago. I was the youngest of four and lived an amazing childhood. I remember at a young age; my parents told me that they were getting a divorce. I did not understand the impact this would have on me at the time. As I got older, I was an excellent student and athlete; life came easy. During my freshman and sophomore years of high school, I started to dabble in alcohol and weed and was arrested twice for underage consumption. My irrational thinking told me, "Maybe I should not drink because I won't be able to pass a breathalyzer, but I can smoke weed and do other drugs because they won't be detected." Boy, was that a crazy thought.

Thus began my downward spiral into more severe drugs, from weed to pills to cocaine. These eventually led me to heroin in my senior year of high school. This story is all too familiar to some. Once I tried heroin, there was no turning back, as it became something my body and mind craved to calm me, to take me away from my disappointment in myself. Snorting heroin quickly turned into shooting heroin, and heroin made those feelings of not belonging and worthlessness all go away…until they came back worse than ever. I began to do everything and anything I could to achieve that next high, and no person, law, or immoral practice would stop me. At the age of 17, I attended my first outpatient rehab. That place offered me support and a plan to find a clean life, but I did not take it seriously because I was 17 years old. I quickly relapsed and began the addiction cycle all over again. This became the pattern of my life, in and out of treatment for the next ten years. I would get sober in the winter by going to a 30-day treatment center, stay sober for the next three months, then dive back deeper into my addiction, and by the end of the year, I would be back in treatment again. For ten years, across states, this was my life. I do not want to go into too many details on this pattern because, well, it gets repetitive, and you get the picture. But I do want to tell you a few stories of what exactly my life looked like during some of the darkest moments of my life in drug addiction.

The first story I want to share with you is how quickly my life spiraled out of control after using drugs or alcohol one time. This story is my example of "one is too many, and a thousand is never enough." In my mid-20s, I had a few months sober, and was living in a halfway house. The World Cup was on and I went to a bar to watch it. Before I knew it, I was multiple beers deep and craving the drug I wanted: heroin. At the time, I was living in Chicago, so I did not have a vehicle. I took two different trains and a bus to make it to my dealer's house. The things we do to get drugs, right? I went about my business and tried to do the previous amount that I did before getting clean. The next thing I remember is waking up in my dealer's house with excruciating pains running down my side. I asked my dealer, "What happened?" His response was, "Well, you OD'd and we had to get you back to life, so we poured boiling water down the side of your body to jump-start your heart" (This was before Narcan was readily available). I lifted my shirt, and I saw the entire left side of my body was blistered and wounded from second-degree burns. I tell you this story because all it takes is one drink or drug to bring you right back into the depths of hell. If you are telling yourself, "I can just have one," "I can control it," or "It won't be like last time," those are lies you are telling yourself. Take it from me. I still have the scars to prove it. These scars are a daily reminder of the life I used to live and how I have been set free from that lifestyle.

This story begins in a jail cell and will show you how I learned the root of all my problems was me, and if I did not work on myself or find a different solution, my problems would always persist. To supply my drug addiction, I had to commit crimes, and these crimes eventually caught up to me. One of the stipulations of my release was that I had to attend treatment and reside in Tennessee for two years. Thus began my two-year journey in Tennessee. Initially, it was an amazing experience and life was good. I had a job, great friends, and a fantastic girlfriend.

The one thing I did not do was work on the issues which caused me to use drugs in the first place. I did not work on the negative feelings inside me and believed I was never going to amount to anything. I did not work on the unresolved issues regarding my parent's divorce, struggles with abandonment, anger, and not ever being good enough. Since I did not work on these issues, guess what happened within three months? Yep, you guessed it—I relapsed in Tennessee and continued my vicious cycle in a completely different state. This eventually led to me losing everything in Tennessee, leaving me homeless and living in my car. I knew if I did not make a change in my life, I was going to die. I was now off my probation. I called my mom crying, and she said I should come back home. So, I packed up my things, said my goodbyes, and started driving back to Chicago while getting high the entire time. It did not matter where I went, who my friends were, how amazing my girlfriend was, or how my family tried to help. If I did not begin to work on <u>my</u> issues within myself, I would continuously stay in this pattern of addiction until I was no longer alive.

This leads me to the "what happened" part of my story. I got back to Chicago, and life did not get any better. This last year before I got sober was the worst pain I have ever experienced, and I am not talking about physical pain. I am talking about complete darkness, filled with guilt, shame, and void of any positivity in my entire mental, emotional, and spiritual health. I brought myself to a new low, where I did not know if I would make it to see tomorrow. It was January 2018, and my mom kicked me out of the house because I woke her up in the middle of the night due to crack psychosis. I remember her crying on the ground in the middle of the hallway with a sheer look of defeat in her eyes. She felt powerless and was at her breaking point. My addiction broke my mom's heart for years, but this time it was different. It was the look of, "My son is going to die, and there is nothing I can do to help him." I will never forget that look – a look of utter defeat and helplessness. My family had done everything they could think of and had given me everything they had to try to help me. But the only one who could help me was God working within me. I packed up my car and was homeless once again. I parked my car in a parking lot for the next couple of days and tried to detox myself. Mind you, it was January in Chicago, so it was about -10 degrees outside. My car had run out of gas, and my cell phone was about to die. I knew I had to decide on what to do, or otherwise, I was going to die out there. I reached out to a recovery advocate I knew and asked him for help. He replied, "Why don't you try South Florida?" I figured eighty degrees and sunny or negative ten degrees and snowing was an easy choice. I packed up my things, said goodbyes to my family, and headed to South Florida on a plane, not realizing how much God was orchestrating my life and bringing me closer to the purpose I longed for.

On January 9th, 2018, upon arriving in Florida and treatment, I was faced with a decision that was going to forever change my life. The decision was, "Do you want to go through the traditional treatment program or attend a faith-based treatment route?" Since I had done the traditional treatment path about 15 times, I figured why not try a faith-based program. That decision was the beginning of my faith journey.

Looking back, I realize now God's voice was inside me that day. It was always there, but only now had I begun to hear it.

In treatment, they took us to Recovery Church Lake Worth and I was in awe. This was a church filled with people who were just like me, broken and hopeless, and they found freedom from addiction through Jesus. This was the first time in my entire life I felt like I belonged. I felt like I was not alone. Looking back, it reminds me of Isaiah 55:8-9, "For my thoughts are not your thoughts, neither are your ways my ways,... As the heavens are higher than the earth, so are my ways higher than your ways and my thoughts than your thoughts." I began to see God was positioning me for my purpose and had brought me to South Florida for a reason.

This sparked a new passion inside of me I had never experienced before. Immediately, I began to dive into Scripture and surrounded myself with Christ-minded people. This led to me meeting my sponsor, a pastor at a local church, and I went through the 12-steps through a Christ-centered lens. I began to learn and feel the unconditional love experienced in a relationship with Christ. Through this love, my selfish heart began to change and I began to think about the needs of others. I began to think of how I could be of maximum service to others. I wanted to become a servant and help others, so I volunteered at Recovery Church every week.

Volunteering alongside people who were just like me was paramount in the transformation which took place in my life. God began to work on some of the deep issues I have struggled with my entire life. He began to shine a mirror on all the issues that used to cause me to turn to a drink or drug and began to heal them one by one. As time went on, I began to look at myself in the mirror again and not recognize who I was. God was transforming me from the inside out, and everything about my life completely changed. My heart had turned from stone into one of loving others and meeting them exactly where they were at. As the *Big Book* tells us, "God was doing for me what I could not do for myself." As my sobriety continued, God continued to do amazing things in me and gave me a sense of self-worth I always wanted. My identity became rooted in Christ, and if I continued to look towards the Father, everything was going to be alright. Concern about opinions or rejection from others began to leave because I know who I am in God's eyes. I belong to a royal priesthood. I am God's masterpiece. I am more than a conqueror. I am chosen and not forsaken. I am important. I am worthy, as He has created me in His image. Leaning into these truths has provided me with the most amazing years of my life and God continues to amaze me every single day.

It is essential to talk about a difficult time in my recovery and spiritual journey because I want to share how God broke a pattern in my life. In May 2020, during the height of COVID, I decided to take a trip back to Chicago to see my family. On this trip, I was not spending time with God and let temptation take over. I was so distant and disconnected from my support and community that I had a relapse. Again, it took one drug, and I woke up in the hospital two days later with the doctor telling me that I should not be alive. At first, I was distraught and felt like a failure until my sponsor called me at the hospital. He encouraged me and reminded me that God is still with me and that everything is going to be okay. The old me would have gone down the rabbit hole and continued in addiction until I lost everything again. This time, being rooted in God and having a strong sense of community, I was able to pick myself back up and stay strong ever since. I firmly believe transformation happens in the context of community. If I did not have a solid foundation in Christ and a strong sense of community, I am not sure if I would have rebounded the way I did after this relapse. Since this relapse, I have dove deeper into my relationship with God, and God has done some amazing things in my life. For the first time, I can say I am happy.

How is my life now? Better than I ever thought possible. I would love to share some of the many blessings that were only possible because of the transformation in me. My transformation is only possible because of my relationship with God. He gets all the glory.

One of the things that plagued me the most was if I was ever going to be loved. Learning and understanding that God's love is enough for me was paramount in my journey. Once I understood God's love is sufficient, then I did not seek it from anywhere else. His love brought me a sense of self-worth and confidence I desperately needed. Only then was I able to find the perfect partner for me. Today, I am happy to say that I am married to my beautiful wife, Hayley. Our marriage was only possible because I learned God loves me, which eventually led to me loving myself.

Another blessing that was only possible through the grace of God is the restored relationships with my family. I was not a pleasant person to be around throughout my addiction, which caused a massive amount of destruction within my family. Though they tried to help me in countless ways through conversations, family counseling and working together to create a plan to help me, it wasn't enough because I was not ready. Worst of all, my relationship with my father deteriorated because of my choices. Today, I have amazing relationships with my family members. God is within me, helping me transform to understand I am a person who is not without flaws but one who is human and part of a family. Many of my family members come to me for guidance or support when going through difficult times. My father is one of my best friends and we finally have the relationship that we both always longed for.

Lastly, my recovery and relationship with Christ have given me a sense of purpose. For so long, I thought and believed that I would never have a real future, but I have been given that today through God. I have recently graduated with a degree in ministry, and I work for Recovery Church Movement. Now I can use my testimony and the gifts God has given me to help others across the nation find freedom from addiction. God will use all the pain I endured for His Glory, and I am humbled to be a part of it. I heard someone once say, "If you are not dead, God is not done," and I am living proof of that.

Ian's Story
The Drop Out ·

Hi, my name is Ian and I'm an addict. I'll start by giving you a little history. I started using around the age of eighteen or nineteen. I quickly realized I was a drug addict and I dropped out of college to pursue my exciting new career as a drug-addicted criminal. The only clean days I had were when I got arrested and had to sit in jail. I would lose them immediately upon my release. Just rinse and repeat that cycle over and over for the next decade or so.

Basically, things weren't going too good for Ian. I'd get put on probation or into some program as an alternative to prison, but I never really gave it 100%. I was also an agnostic at the time, so my higher power of nature, or a doorknob, or whatever I picked that time around, really wasn't helping me stay clean. Don't get me wrong, I like nature and all, but it doesn't really have much of an agenda for you, and it didn't help me stop using drugs. I didn't have anything against religion, I just thought it wasn't for me. I didn't want any more rules to follow or be controlled by anything. Ironically, my life was being completely controlled by drugs.

So, this last go around, when things went south as they usually do when you're using large amounts of drugs daily, I got desperate and decided to pray. At this point, I figured what's the harm. The circumstances of my life began to change; not in ways I wanted, but in ways I needed. I got a DUI and went to jail, which was the only way I was going to quit at that point. I met Pastor S learned about this Christian-based recovery program. I decided I needed to make a change and put some work into staying sober and should learn more about the God I had chosen to ignore my whole life. So, throughout my time in that program and in jail, I started building a personal relationship with a God of my understanding.

I surrounded myself with like-minded supportive people who are also committed to staying clean and doing the work, and what do you know, it's worked. I have a great sponsor who's agreed to take me through the steps. I'm currently working through step four. I've been clean for about 21 months now. I've graduated from the treatment program and life is good. I'm clean. I owe it all to trusting in God and trusting people who have faith in God. Thanks for letting me share.

Beth's Story
The Mother of an Addict

I prayed faithfully, fasted some, and believed God for the miracle of healing our son. I asked in Jesus' name and for His Glory. Surely God would do a great miracle. The miracle I planned in my mind was not what occurred. But as I look back over Jimmy's life, I know God was with us every step of the way… answering prayers along the way. Never give up and never stop praying for your loved one.

Our son's addiction started over ten years ago. At first, we just believed he would grow out of it. He was a very smart kid…top ten percent of his class, and he attended one of the top colleges in Virginia. He was athletic, tall, good-looking, and had a beautiful smile. His addiction started his senior year of high school, possibly from a back injury with pain medicine and eventual experimental drugs. The addiction only accelerated partying through four years of college. He came back home after his fourth year of college to work. With more money in hand and opioids on the rise, his life quickly spiraled out of control. Opioids were becoming more popular on the party scene and even though Jimmy did not grow up as a risk taker, partying gave him that edge to be more risky. Jimmy believed he could have fun and stop when it was time for life to get more serious.

As parents, we were in the middle of chaos. There were so many incidents of police, fights within the household, drug dealers dropping off drugs in our driveway, car accidents……you name it! There never seemed to be a peaceful moment.

We were finally able to use our leverage as parents and get him into the residential drug program at the church where my husband was on staff as a pastor. After a pending court date, they removed him from the church program and put him into a local secular program with which the court system had a relationship. This was disappointing, but he was able to experience several months of sobriety until he entered into a relationship as a codependent wounded person with no coping skills. I think he really just wanted to get that great job and a wife and move on with life. However, he was unwilling to take the time to do the work to become healthy, and so this cycle continued over the next several years. His drug issues also continued to escalate. There were bouts of homelessness and even a short stint in jail. He would continue bouncing in and out of treatment programs and sober living for the next few years of his life. Thankfully a couple of programs in Florida introduced him to Calvary Chapel. Through the ups and downs, he would find peace in the times he attended that church.

As time passed, my husband became our church's Director of the Recovery Program. He was in long-term recovery himself. God continued to work on me as well. Our church program opened up opportunities for me to partner with my husband in the ministry. I came to know and love so many of those impacted by this awful disease, which also included many affected by human trafficking. Relationships with others in recovery helped me to understand and love my son through the good and bad. Finding a supportive parents group helped me to cope in a healthier way and set healthy boundaries for myself. I learned to encourage my son in his recovery instead of trying to control the things that were out of my control. Our son knew he was loved by us until his final breath. Our phone calls always ended with "I love you."

We met Phil and were introduced to the Recovery Church Movement several years ago. We were looking for a class at a seminar, got lost, and ended up at his table. Really God sent us there. From the moment we met Phil, we knew he was the real deal, and this movement was special and much needed in the recovery world. Over the past few years, we have been able to spend time with Phil and get to know him better. We were able to finally attend a leadership conference this past October. The weekend we spent with those in recovery and involved in the RCM was a mountain top experience. We spent a long weekend worshiping with many whose lives were changed by the power of Jesus. My son would have greatly benefited from a group like this. He would have had a community to grow in Christ and do life with. He would have had a home and family.

On June 19, 2021, as I ran to the local grocery store, I was listening to a CD. A wave of peace almost knocked me over. It was stronger than any peace I'd experienced before. I was alone in my car, but out loud, I said, "Thank you. I don't know what that was for but thank you." A couple of hours after returning home, we received the worst news of our lives. Our son, Jimmy, died of an opioid overdose. God did not answer my prayers the way we wanted or expected. But He was there. He went before us and sent His peace. Deuteronomy 31:8 reminds me of that morning. "Do not fear or be dismayed... The LORD Himself goes before you; He will be with you. He will never leave you nor forsake you. Do not be afraid or discouraged."

As a parent, we never give up or stop praying and believing God is working. He did work through the ups and downs of my son's life. The prayers many prayed for him were not in vain. Many divine appointments showed up for us and for him though these long years. He had many victories along the way. God's hand was in his life until the very end. He was actually doing well before his death and after a brutal struggle through 2020 and the pandemic. He was working, enjoying life, and back to church. We even had a peer send a note mentioning Jimmy's faith got him back to God and back to church. That was a treasure to hold onto. In the midst of the past year, God has provided what we needed when we needed it.

We miss Jimmy terribly, and we think of him every single day. His smile would light up a room. I can't say I like God's plan at all, but I trust His plan, and I trust Him completely. God is always faithful, and He has not left our side since that day. As crazy as it seems, my faith in Him has increased. I know we must continue to glorify God and share His love and hope with others fighting this battle. He will provide the strength we need for each day…one day at a time.

Meggan's Story
The Dope Fiend

I'm 41 years old and have been an addict for 64% of my life. Growing up in Akron, Ohio, I had a great childhood. I had two older sisters and a younger brother. My mom was a single parent, sometimes working three jobs to ensure we lived in good neighborhoods with good schools. She didn't want us struggling the way she did. My grandparents were still alive, and I would spend entire weekends with them going to garage sales and to the library. I developed a lifelong love of books, thanks to my grandmother. I would go to church with them every Sunday. I also loved, loved going to Bible camp. I could always tell when camp was coming up because my mom would pick up an extra shift or job so that my brother and I could go. Life was good.

Let's fast forward a couple of years. When I was fifteen and my brother fourteen, we found out that we were both products of an affair. My dad was always around on the weekends, and we just assumed it was normal he wasn't there all the time since my parents were never married. At about the same time, I started smoking pot with friends in high school. These choices eventually led to me skipping the end-of-year finals and getting held back. I was officially a freshman again and in the same homeroom as my little brother! You would think that I would be embarrassed, but I wasn't. By my second round of ninth grade, I was into raves and steadily doing more hard-core drugs. Cocaine became my one love. I put my mom through hell for a couple of years. I was kicked out and forced to live with one of my sisters, suspended too many times to count. I was told I wouldn't graduate, so I got myself somewhat together, took summer classes and classes from home, and graduated when I was in eleventh grade with a technical degree in Culinary Arts and Catering. When I was in second grade, my mother had me tested, and I had a twelfth grade reading level. I was always bright; I just never applied it once I started using drugs. My drug usage continued getting worse and worse. I started using meth, drinking, and continued with cocaine. My brother Michael and oldest nephew Zack started using and going to raves with me.

When I was twenty-five, and Michael was twenty-four, we both got jobs as Journeyman Apprentice for a company my mother worked for. We were making good money. My mom was traveling a lot for work, and she had been in California teaching engineering for the past three months. My sister Jennifer had moved to Florida a month earlier, and my sister Kelly was camping with her family for the week somewhere in Ohio. My brother and I had a long week of overtime. A storm had come through a couple of different townships, and telephone poles had been taken out, so a lot of people had no power. Once we finally got a day off, we spent the day relaxing and watching movies. Around six, Michael smoked a joint and went to sleep. He never woke again. I don't want to get into all the details of that day, but I can say to this day that this was the worst day of my life. While my brother was sleeping, I invited some friends over. We had been doing cocaine and drinking all night. I was too high to realize my brother had quit breathing. When I realized what was going on, I called 911 and started CPR. I had no idea what I was doing, but I continued till the paramedics came. They took him to the nearest hospital. I didn't even follow them right away; I needed to put a couple more lines in me, followed by more beer. Who does that?

I got to walk into room 1 of that hospital and see my Michael dead. They had cut his clothes off, and he still had the ET tube coming out of his mouth, pads from where they tried to jumpstart his heart. I don't know how long I spent in that room with him. I'm not even sure how I got home that day. In between doing more lines and drinking, I spent hours trying to get a hold of my family. I saved my mom for last because I knew that would be the hardest phone call. I have nightmares about the sound that came from her. The next couple of days were a blur of cocaine and alcohol. I went to my Michael's funeral high as a kite and wailed the loudest in the front row. I couldn't face what had happened, and I couldn't comfort my mom. I blamed myself for not being able to save him because I was too high. This heavy load of guilt and shame took me down a fifteen-year rabbit hole of darkness.

I met a guy named Steve the same day my brother died. He's the one who introduced me to crack. For all the shame and guilt, I felt for not saving Michael, I thought I deserved the beatings, the name-calling that Steve dealt out to me. I took it for years. I let Steve open credit cards in my brother's name, and I did the same thing to my mother, all so I could smoke crack and drink. My mother moved to Florida; she couldn't stay in the house where my brother died. In 2008 I found out I was pregnant. I quit everything until two months after I gave birth to my beautiful daughter Addison. I went right back to it; my life was full of self-loathing and anger. One of the neighbors reported me to child services due to my screaming whenever Steve would start hitting me. I failed a drug test, and they took my daughter from me. I quit drugs again and went to every class required of me. Steve was useless during all this.

The first night Addison was allowed to stay at home, Steve was angry I wouldn't give him my only five dollars. So, while holding our daughter, he punched me in the face and threw me to the ground. I got to our bedroom and locked the door; I called the cops, and for the first time in four years, I pressed charges. Once he was arrested, I called my mother and asked her for help. She flew to Ohio from Florida. I called child services and told them the situation and that I wanted to leave Ohio. They gave me back my daughter. My mother and I had my apartment packed in one week, and we were on our way to Clearwater, Florida.

I was still drinking with my sister and her husband, but I didn't know anyone, so I didn't have access to any drugs. I did eventually find a bar down the street. I made some friends and what do you think happened? I found the drugs I was craving. I decided to go to paramedic school to help people. I didn't want anyone to go through what I had with Michael. I graduated top of my class. No one knew I spent all my money on drugs and alcohol. I was taking home random men from the bar to have sex. I would sneak them into the house, knowing my daughter and mother were sleeping upstairs. I didn't give a thought about anything happening; luckily, nothing ever did.

I was a paramedic for a while until I met Sean in 2013. He introduced me to Molly (ecstasy), which was the first thing I ever shot up. I was also introduced to my now husband Steve. He was an opiate addict several times over. I was introduced to pills. I quit drinking at this point because it took away from the money I needed for pills. I moved in with Steve in 2015. We both still maintained some sort of life at this point. We both had jobs. Whatever money I didn't spend on pills and cocaine was spent on Addison. I would send her back to Ohio for the summers so she could be with her grandmother from her paternal side and my oldest sister Kelly, plus all my nephews and nieces. I was arrested in 2016 for burglary. I don't remember exactly what happened, but I woke up in jail. This arrest would be the start of a trend of racking up felonies. Addison's grandmother Linda got awarded custody of Addison while I was in jail. I found out and thought to hell with it. I've got nothing left. Who the hell cares about me anyway? I didn't have Addison anymore; I could do whatever I wanted. And I did.

For the next five years, it was a revolving door of getting arrested for drugs, credit card fraud, and dealing in stolen property. Steve and I were eventually kicked out of his mom's house, and we were homeless for four years. We were offered a place to stay either because people knew we had drugs on us and wanted that form of payment, or they knew I had access to many dealers. I worked hard at being homeless. Instead of getting help, I chose to continue being homeless and gamble with my life every time I stuck a needle in my arm. I ended up overdosing five times during this time in my life. Thanks to God, Steve was able to bring me back every time.

In 2019 I was in jail for ten months, Steve dumped me, and I tried to overdose on purpose. My friend Travis saved my life. I had had trouble breathing for a couple of days and thought it would be better if the pain was gone. While in jail, it was my job to clean the black mold. I ended up with pneumonia and was in the hospital for weeks with a chest tube. I almost died. At this point, I had basically forgotten that I had a daughter and barely spoke to her. I went home to Ohio after I was discharged. I got to see her for the first time in three years. It was a very bittersweet moment. I left her that day and went back to my sister's house. I got high and ended up ODing yet again. I was transported to the nearest hospital. Thanks to Narcan, I was awake at that point, and wouldn't you know it; they tried to put me in the same room in which Michael had died. I started freaking out. My family couldn't believe what I had become. I hated and blamed God for all wrongs in my life. If he hadn't taken my brother from me, my life would have been so much better. I'm so glad I don't feel this way anymore. I came back to Florida and jumped right back into a relationship with another man who liked to hit women. I got him addicted to Fentanyl.

You might be wondering what happened to Steve. He had decided to get help. He moved to Delray Beach and went into treatment. We spoke the whole time I was with the other man. Steve got insurance and got connected in the sober community in his area. Steve made some calls and got me insurance and into a great treatment center. He paid for my greyhound bus ticket to Delray Beach. I actually got on that bus. I was sick and tired of being sick and tired. I went to a treatment center in Lake Worth, FL. I will forever be grateful to all the staff, techs and my therapist Susan. They saved my life. Susan helped me get over my guilt and shame over Michael. Susan helped me to forgive myself. Michael's autopsy never revealed a cause of death. The toxicology report showed he had pot in his system and nothing else. This year will be the sixteenth anniversary of Michael's death. I will never get over the loss of my brother, but the hole in my heart has slowly healed.

So, I get out of treatment and do what every addict in recovery does. I got a sponsor and a home group down in Miami. I lied about how much clean time I had so I could get a job at a detox center. I wanted to help people. Steve and I had rekindled our relationship. I got tired of seeing him once a month since I lived in Miami. Steve gave me the phone number for Kentucky Dave. Dave is a house manager for a recovery house. He helped open the door for me to move to Boynton Beach. I moved into the women's house, and within a week, I was hired at a treatment facility as a BHT. I started off on the third shift due to not having a license. But with hard work and a love for helping people, I've gotten promoted to first shift and a group facilitator.

Now on to how I came back to God. My sponsor had me describe who and what my Higher Power was. I was still on the borderline about God. But I have a love for Star Wars, so my higher power was Obi One Kenobi, but it looked and sounded like Ewan McGregor. This worked for a while and helped me through my steps. Steve has always been religious; he was raised Catholic. He really got into going to this thing called Recovery Church in Delray Beach and The Avenue Church. So, like every good girlfriend, I started going to church with him because I knew he loved it. The minute I walked into the doors of RC Delray, I knew I had found my place and people. I have never been more welcomed anywhere in my life. RC Delray has a truly amazing group of people serving. Thanks to the family I gained there, I started serving at RC Delray and The Avenue Church. I signed up for every class and always said yes to helping out in some function. I signed up for Disciples Making Disciples through Recovery Church Movement and got to go to the leadership conference. I was baptized in the ocean on September 4th, 2021, and was proposed to by Steve that same night. Through all my trials and tribulations, I have come to truly love and believe in God again and found my purpose in helping addicts and alcoholics find hope. There's no place I'd rather be on a Monday night than at Recovery Church Delray Beach. My name is Meggan, and I'm a grateful recovering addict, thanks to God and my RC family.

John's Story
The Worshiper

My parents tell me that I would always overeat when I was a baby. You guys, I have had this thing for a very, very long time. A disease of "As long as certain conditions are met, I will be happy." If it made me feel good, I wanted more of it. I remember going to ridiculous lengths to get what I wanted. Like most kids, I loved sugar. If there were none in the form of candy or cookies that I could sneak extra of, I would literally climb onto the counter, retrieve the container of raw sugar, and quickly pour as much as I could fit into my mouth, then sneak off to a quiet corner to enjoy my spoils.

Growing up, I NEVER could save any money. I don't remember how much of an allowance we were given. Two bucks a week, maybe? If I got the money on Friday, I would be broke on Saturday. Buying some cheap toy or bag of candy. Meanwhile, I would watch my brother amass this wad of cash, both wondering why he did it and how he did it. Until recently, the concepts of "delayed gratification" and "good things come to those who wait" were utterly lost on me. I learned pretty early on that if the rules could be successfully bypassed, they didn't truly apply to me. I could have what I wanted, when I wanted it, provided I managed my dishonesty and subversive tactics well. If I wasn't lying to my parents and teachers, I was lying to myself in the form of rationalization and justification.

Fast forward a bit to when I first discovered alcohol and its effects. I was in love! I was fifteen or sixteen when I came across my first opportunity to sample the stuff. In the Doctor's Opinion, it says, "Men and women drink essentially because they like the effect produced by alcohol." I loved how it made me feel. It gave me this sense of freedom and adventure that I had been craving. By the age of eighteen, I was hiding bottles of vodka in the crawlspace of the house. There are probably still empty bottles there to this day.

I remember vividly my father asking if I would like to come with him on this overseas trip. What an opportunity! Of course, I would go. But how was I going to get to sleep? How would I calm my nerves? The obsession that most of you are all too familiar with had begun to set in. During the trip, I would take any and every opportunity to drink.

From a very early age, I knew God was real, that he loved me, and that I could have a relationship with Him. I am very grateful to have been raised in the environment that I was. I experienced many powerful God moments growing up. I was sure He was real; however, I felt He was all about rules and regulations. "Can't have sex before marriage." "Honor your father and mother." "Don't do insane amounts of methamphetamine and burn your life to the ground." You know, rules... Once again, rules were simply guidelines for folks who didn't have the smarts to break them and get away with it. I thought to follow God, I had to follow the rules. I have since found out that once I decided to surrender to His relentless pursuit of my heart, it is, in fact, the other way around. It is by following Christ I am able to and have the desire to follow the rules.

I'm going to save you guys the gory details of my alcoholism and addiction. You know the story, though, and if you don't know the story, I bet you're familiar with the feelings attached to it. Shame, deep shame from having lost parental rights to my daughter, broke my wife's heart, worried my family sick, lost the respect of my friends, cared more about whether my girlfriend was cheating on me with the dope man than if my daughter felt safe, spent my retirement, borrowed $15,000 with no intention of ever paying it back, spent untold hours picking at my skin, lost several jobs, took my motorcycle apart and never put it back together, experienced psychosis so bad I could no longer distinguish reality from the nightmare playing out in my mind... I could increase this list ad-infinitum.

Ladies and Gentlemen, this was the culmination of me playing God. These things all came about in my life because I insisted on taking the path of least resistance. I insisted that responsibility and integrity were only ideals I needed to know how to fake, not practically apply. I insisted that I was a kind and loving human being but found no compassion, grace, or mercy for myself. And only found some for others when I felt good enough to give it. I was living like a scared animal, backed into a corner of his own making, shrieking in terror as the mirrors closed in on him. I had no money, no friends, no sanity, no peace. I just hurt all the time. I came to a choice... Either continue with the way I was living, which I knew in my heart meant death or permanent insanity, or simply surrender to the One who had been faithfully pursuing my heart from the very beginning.

Revelation 3:20 says, "Behold, I stand at the door, and knock: if any man hear my voice, and open the door, I will come into him, and will dine with him and he with me." By this time, Jesus had worn a hole through my door and was peeking in and gently saying, "You good? You had enough?" The *Big Book* talks about being beaten into a state of reasonableness. I can relate.

I had been to a state-run treatment center before, and by the end of my stay there I thought I had surrendered. I was praying. I was reading the *Big Book* and the Bible. I was going to meetings and got a sponsor when I got home. I even started working the steps. But, as it would turn out, I had not fully surrendered. I wanted to hang on to this unhealthy relationship with my girlfriend. I was getting high again shortly after getting ninety days sober.

Christ was calling me to an unconditional surrender. I'm certain I completed much of the heart of steps one through three on the plane ride down here. I would follow wherever He would lead, no matter the cost, no matter the hit to my pride, no matter having to completely unlearn life and let Him teach me a new way to live. I vividly remember sitting on the back stoop of a treatment center and praying fervently that he let me keep my girlfriend. You know that she would find real, sustained sobriety, and we could live "happily ever after." The response I heard in my heart was very clear, "I need your undivided attention right now. We have work to do." I broke up with her over the phone later that evening.

I wish I could tell you at this point I remained sober. I did not. In terms of time, I put together a little over nine months, went through my steps, and had even begun sponsoring other guys. I got a great job working for Amazon. They sent me down for training in Miami. I got very bored and very lonely. At first, I was doing what my sponsor suggested I do. Go to a meeting every day, call five other drunks a day, and pray every chance I got. But after the third or fourth week of this, I slacked off. Shortly thereafter, on my way back to the hotel after a stressful day of training, I decided I was going to get high. Who would know? I could get away with it. There was no defense.

For the next few months, I struggled. I went to treatment a few more times and got booted from my halfway house. I was living at the Motel 6 on Lantana. Psychosis had returned. My friends and my parents were worried about me. I was quickly running out of money. Again, I found myself struggling to determine reality from the voices in my mind. This insanity was no way to live, and I knew it. I knew it because I had, through God's grace, experienced some freedom. I had experienced some real joy in my life. Philippians 4:7 says, "Be anxious for nothing, but in everything by prayer and supplication, with thanksgiving, let your requests be made known to God; and the peace of God, which surpasses all understanding, will guard your hearts and minds through Christ Jesus." I had learned first-hand EXACTLY what that verse was referencing.

I knew what to do. I surrendered again. I spent one more

night in that hotel room, no more drugs, but definitely not sane or sober. I got up the next day and made some phone calls. I went to a men's meeting that night. On my way to that meeting was when I had a profound spiritual experience. The best way I can describe this, at least for some of you older folks, is to imagine scrolling through the channels on an old radio with an analog tuner. The static and barely intelligible voices were interrupted with a voice that came through loud and clear. A beautiful voice, a familiar voice. I knew immediately in my heart of hearts this was my father's voice. Probably one of the most eloquent prayers I had ever heard.

To this day, I wish I had pulled over to the side of the road to write it down. Tears were streaming down my face. This seemed SO real. Like he was sitting next to me in the truck and the Spirit of the Lord and a whole host of angels there also. Even if this was a figment of my imagination, it was the most encouraging and uplifting figment ever. Just as abruptly as it began, it stopped. It stirred up in me such an intense well of emotions, both for my father and my God, I decided to call him and tell him exactly what I had experienced. That's when he informed me he, my mom, and my sister had just finished praying for me. And I had just recounted, word for word, the prayer for me he had just prayed. I was flabbergasted. At that moment, I knew several things without a shadow of any doubt:

1. God is Real, as real as you and I are here on this planet and has the power to bridge space and time to perform miracles.

2. He loves me so much. Enough to connect me with my father over a thousand miles of distance in a time when I felt so scared and alone. Enough to bend the standard rules that apply here on this earth. Enough to send his only Son, the Christ, the Word made flesh, to die a brutal death, that through him we may not only have life but have it abundantly. John 10:10 reads, "The thief comes

only to steal and kill and destroy; I came that they may have life and have it abundantly."

3. He has a purpose for my life. Just as he intervened when dark forces threatened to consume me, he calls me to do the same for others. To be a light. To be an ambassador. Matthew 4:19 "And He said to them, "Follow Me, and I will make you fishers of men."

Don't be surprised when he puts you to work. God wastes nothing, and him rescuing you from dark forces, dark chemicals, and your own sin and depravity is no accident. He has a purpose and a calling on your life; make no mistake. The fact that you are reading this now is direct evidence of this personal invitation. I can speak with authority on this matter because a similar thing happened to me. In June of 2020, Pastor Mitch from Recovery Church reached out to me, and we sat down for coffee. He stated he felt God led him to ask if I would be interested in leading worship for Recovery Church Delray. Every hair on my body stood on end. Me? Lead something? Surely you have the wrong guy. I had a little over three months sober. The only thing on my resume that would qualify me for this position is my time spent as a guitarist in a rock and roll band. I knew how to play music at seedy bars for seedy people, but worship music for recovering addicts and alcoholics? What a blessing this has been to me. To be allowed to use the gifts and talents God gave me to bring glory to His name is an experience not to be missed. What gifts and talents do you have that God is calling you to employ for His kingdom?

Jessica's Story
The "ZOOM baby"

Seven hundred ninety days ago, I woke my husband from a dead sleep at two A.M. With these words, I AM AN ALCOHOLIC, and I need help. From that moment on, I knew my old way of life was about to change. However, I just didn't know how or if it was possible. I just knew God was in control because I was powerless over alcohol. My addiction to alcohol had become so severe that I needed to be medically detoxed, and to this day, I have not discussed my detox with anyone but my family and my sponsor.

Over time life became harder and harder. I became more lonely, depressed, and defeated. This was only increased by my growing alcohol intake. I started drinking, like many others, with just a glass of wine to enjoy in the evening and progressed all the way to parties where drinking was the primary focus. I started noticing everything in my life revolved around drinking. I progressed from binge drinking on the weekends to drinking daily from one glass of wine to an entire bottle of wine, to a box of wine, and when the box of wine was not enough to get me through the day, a bottle of vodka was added to the mix. I was drinking to keep the shaking away and numb my past feelings.

I was what they call a high-functioning alcoholic. As a "functioning alcoholic," I worked and lived apparently successfully, skillfully, and effectively, despite having alcohol continuously in my body, derailing my behavior and emotions. Yet, I have many clients today who have no idea that I am an alcoholic or the amount of alcohol that ran through my system daily.

My story is the typical story of many alcoholics. A story I never thought was MY STORY or a story that was not even notable. But here I am, trying to put into words my story to help others. I am a woman of many words, but one who's struggling to write this... I'm a woman, a wife, a mother, a friend, a boss, a caregiver, and an alcoholic. I'm a lot of things, to a lot of people, or so I thought. But most importantly, a child of GOD.

After completing a week in detox, my husband signed me out. We had not even spoken during the week. Life was scrolling through my head. I was scared, lost, and to say I was nervous was an understatement. The ride home with my husband alone made me think my whole decision to get help was wrong. However, I remember getting a folder in detox with some paperwork in it. I also remember in detox being told ninety meetings in ninety days and to get a sponsor. Words that stuck. So, as I sat in my office, overwhelmed, confused, and with my head spinning. I opened this yellow folder where I found a paper that didn't say A.A. It said RECOVERY CHURCH. My gut told me to make the call and ask them for help.

Within days of getting out of detox, I had a sponsor, and then the pandemic, lockdowns, and all that came with it hit hard. Instantly, there were no in-person meetings, NOT that I knew what that was anyhow. I just knew I was supposed to go to these meetings. So now what? My first sponsor contacted me and instructed me to contact her every day for thirty days and relay what you are doing to stay sober. That's all the assignments I had thus far. But the pandemic was now in full swing.

I was given a ZOOM code to go online to a meeting through Recovery Church. All of this was a foreign language to me. In addition, I'm not a very technical person. But I did find Recovery Church Online was something I could do from anywhere - at work, home, or in the car. I found that connecting with others like me was helpful. I discovered that ZOOMING daily was helping my recovery. My first zoom meeting was terrifying. How do I introduce myself? What do I even say? All the standard NEWBIE questions and fears had set in. Within my first meeting, I started hearing all the one-liners: "Ninety meetings in ninety days," "One day at a time," and "Keep coming back." All the stuff "old-timers" would say drove me crazy, to say the least. I hated to hear the slogans shared. But it seemed like every day, I would ZOOM in, and it was a cleanse of my emotions. I cried almost every meeting for the first year. I shook like a leaf in the wind when I was called upon to share. Others, with sobriety time under their belt, would say, "It's ok," "Keep coming back," "Newcomers keep us sober," and they promised me "the crying will not last forever." More "quotes" I hated in the beginning, mostly because I was so self-absorbed, and I thought I was the only one with true problems. However, each time I would attend an online Recovery Church Meeting, it seemed more and more like something I could do. I *could* stay sober and fit it into my schedule whenever. This had to be doable, right? I didn't want to go back to the life I was living. I was willing to do anything to not be "that drunk."

I found listening to other's stories similar to my own strangely comforting. I found opening up and telling "my story" seemed scary and yet somehow helpful. I found it comforting to know I was not alone. At this point in the pandemic, all of Recovery Church was online. There were meetings every day. I found this helpful to connect with others in the program. As "My Story' started to evolve - first thirty days sober, then ninety days, then one year. All milestones beyond my wildest dreams. The work was hard, but here I am, over two years later, exclusively doing Recovery Church via online meetings and doing it ONE DAY AT A TIME.

As the pandemic was coming to the point of things opening back up, I heard rumors of in-person meetings opening back up. Anxiety set in. My emotions were all over the place. Thinking of the upcoming changes and how I would miss "my people" online scared me. Changes for me were about to happen, or so I thought. Change is not something I do well. I begged my online homegroup not to go away. I was scared I would be left alone, with nowhere to go. Something I have had deep-rooted fears of due to my childhood, my narcissistic mother, my lack of knowing my biological father, and being an only child, even if I wasn't spoiled like one.

I had never attended an in-person meeting. How could I do this? What would the people be like? Other than detox, Recovery Church was all I knew. After about two years of sobriety, I was given the nickname "ZOOM baby" because I had gotten sober online. So, it seems "my story" was a little different from others, but it was all I knew. I didn't see it, but it was pointed out by other members of RC they thought getting sober only online was incredible, like some great accomplishment. Humbled, I didn't want to see it or draw attention to myself because "Hello," I'm still human, and what if I messed up? What if I fell off the wagon? All the emotions were setting in, but it was true. I was what they considered a ZOOM BABY. Someone who solely got sober online. Something new. I, however, didn't know anything different.

I got completely sober in Recovery Church Online via Zoom. Through RC, I have become a leader in our online group and volunteer my time to chair meetings, lead open share, give scripture and testimonies, and help with the planning and themes of our online meetings. I have even attended a Recovery Church leadership conference in Nashville. The conference exposed me to the whole picture of the Recovery Church Movement and all it entails, including the many campuses across the country. I fell absolutely in love with the movement and the mission behind Recovery Church of helping the drug addict and alcoholic find both recovery and Jesus. I love how my recovery can be combined and complemented by my relationship with Jesus. I have attended our yearly planning weekend at Harvey Cedars Christian camp in NJ for our online campus. In addition, I found my forever sponsor - someone in Recovery Church who had seen me from the beginning, someone who understood me. I was delighted!!

Recovery Church has brought so many blessings in sobriety. Speaking and telling "my story" is not something I ever thought I'd do, but I am honored that I can tell "HIS story" of sobriety through Recovery Church. It is very therapeutic in my recovery journey to be open, honest, and transparent. I have watched GOD transform my life. After years of feeling incomplete, I have finally become the woman I believe God intended. The challenge for me now is not to fight the urge to drink. It's now about continuing to grow on spiritual terms and stay passionate about my recovery. Now my journey is about consistently seeking. Looking for ways to help others, seeking the truth, and living it. This journey is now about staying humble and teachable. It's about doing the next faithful thing regardless of the consequences.

Let me close by thanking my family, my God, and Recovery Church for, without them, I would not be where I am today. Thank you and God Bless.

Gina's Story
The Child of Alcoholics

My name is Gina, and I am in recovery from drugs, alcohol, and a life of escape fueled by self will run riot. I am an adult child of two duel diagnosed alcoholics, and I was raised in the rooms of Alcoholics Anonymous. When I was younger, I didn't realize how much of a blessing that was; to be honest, I viewed it more as a curse. As I grew in sobriety and the Lord, I realized how blessed I was; I knew where to go, and that is something I took for granted for far too long.

My whole life, up until around the age of eighteen, my parents were in sobriety, and when I was young, we were pretty involved in church. My mom was a youth leader, and we were there every Sunday. That is until some things happened, and we left. From that point forward, I would occasionally go to other churches with my friends but never really got involved. However, I started going to a youth group that was not affiliated with a church for a little while, which I loved.

Around the same time (middle school), my mental health issues started to surface. I started cutting myself and acting out. A friend at school told a teacher about my cutting, and they sent me to see the school counselor. Long story short, she told me I was safe and could be honest and then went and told my parents everything I had said; enter trust issues. I was taken to a psychiatrist and prescribed medication and counseling. Back then, I had dabbled in some of the more "elementary" drugs and drinking, but it never really took hold.

Amid all of this, I fell in love with someone of the same gender and was ostracized. The people that told me God loved me just the way I was now had a different view, and I started to really rebel. In my eighth and ninth grade years, I was getting into so much trouble that my mom threatened to send me to a Christian school or put me in cyber school if I didn't leave my home school and go to our local Vo-Tech. So, in tenth grade, off to Vo-Tech I went. The remainder of high school was pretty uneventful. Aside from the ever-continuing battle with my mental health, I no longer dabbled with drugs and alcohol and trouble, and I was an honor roll student.

In the years directly after high school, my mental health was at its worst, and I hit low after low. I couldn't hold a job, and by the age of nineteen, I was fighting for disability. Right before my twenty-first birthday, I had yet another breakdown, promptly followed by yet another inpatient stay. I moved to Tennessee, where my parents had relocated a few years prior. When I got home, my boyfriend, whom I lived with, dumped me. At this point, both of my parents were off the wagon and drinking all the time already, and then my now-husband came to live with us, and along with him came the addition of his drug use. In drinking and drugging, I found my calling. I found freedom from the dungeon that was my own mind. I started to use, and I actually felt normal. We partied a lot in those first two years of our relationship, and I had finally found my place in the world. Everyone seemed to love me, I didn't hurt, and nothing mattered.

In 2012 my now husband and I moved back to Pennsylvania from Tennessee so we could find jobs and start living an "adult" life. At this point, I assumed all the partying was circumstantial, and I didn't have any inkling I might have a problem yet. The day after we drove back to PA, we got the call that there was an accident, and my seventeen-year-old little brother was in a coma. That night he died from head trauma caused by "hood surfing" (hanging on the hood of a car while someone drove around). Something in me died with him. I helped raise him. We (my brothers and I) came second to the program, and that left us home to fend for ourselves a lot. My older brother to look after me once he was old enough, and me to look after my younger brother once I was old enough. As if I wasn't already mad enough at God, now I hated him. How could he do that? How could he rip my family apart? My older brother was in Afghanistan at the time and had to find out via email. Why God? Those were the only words I could muster, and with them, I completely turned my back on God. As if I wasn't already drinking and drugging to escape, now I didn't want to ever feel again.

Fast forward a couple of years and a lot of mess, and we have friends who, of course, drink like we do. We hung out with this one couple all of the time. She was my best friend, and he was my husband's best friend. One night he raped me. He broke my final piece. The one last part of me that hung on to any sanity, any hope, and it was gone. After that, things got really dark for me. I hid it for three years from everyone. We continued to hang out with that couple and my husband. Everyone else in my life couldn't figure out why I was unraveling at the seams. I hated myself. I hated the world, and I just wanted it to be over. The drinking and drugs no longer provided that escape I so desperately longed for. I dreamt of the release of death. I never really wanted to die, just to cease to exist, but that was the only way I could think to make that happen. Instead of killing myself, which seemed like too permanent of a solution, I figured I would do what I had seen people do my whole life. I tried to get sober.

I went to rehab and "tried" working a program. One of the biggest things about the program is that it is God-focused. With my history with God, I didn't want anything to do with that. I got out of rehab, and after about three months of "working a program," I stopped going and decided I could do it on my own (This was not my first attempt at getting sober, mind you). As you'll notice, the word "tried" and the statement "working a program" are both in quotation marks; that is because these days, I know better. These days, I know that "half measures avail us NOTHING." (*Big Book* of Alcoholics Anonymous, How It Works, p. 59) I made it about a year and a half, dry, not sober. I found out my husband was doing meth during that time, and I wound up moving out. I was still trying to hide all my demons, and they were really getting the best of me. Eventually, I gave up, I moved home, and, as they say, I couldn't beat them, so I joined them. Finally, one night I had enough, and all tuned up in the midst of a bender, I let it rip.

Everything I had been hiding in one, not so graceful pile of word vomit came flowing out at my unsuspecting husband. I regretted that for a really long time. I didn't regret telling him; it had to come out eventually, but the way I went about it. Hurting my husband that way, spewing that sort of toxicity, and completely blindsiding him after hiding it for so long. That was my rock bottom. My husband's rock bottom came about two days later when he put a freshly cleaned and fully loaded hunting rifle in his mouth and pulled the trigger. The gun jammed, and it was there that we found God. He went to the hospital that night and to rehab the next day, and I cleaned out the house.

Our sobriety date is January 21st, 2020. When we got sober, I still really struggled with "the God thing." I came to terms there absolutely was a God. I just didn't want to attribute this miracle to "The God." I tried to find God in everything and found everything wanting. But a funny thing happens when you're desperate enough, you become willing. I was willing to go to any lengths to get and stay sober, and I desperately wanted a new life. I knew the program worked. I had seen it time and time again. So I was, as they told me to be, honest, open, and willing.

My husband got there a lot faster than I did. While I dabbled in everything I could get my hands on, including tarot, astrology, Wiccan practices, etc., he started going to church, and I saw a change happening in him, one that wasn't happening in me. He started playing "Jesus" music, which made me cringe, but it made him happy. He would read scripture, and my skin would crawl, but he was really into it. Man was the devil on me!

The name Jesus truly terrifies him, and the thought of losing his grip on us is beyond what he can handle. My husband kept trying to drag me to church, but I wasn't that willing yet. I even volunteered to work on Sundays to have a reason not to go. Eventually, though, he got me, and I went to church with him one Sunday. I just wept the whole time. After that, I decided I would go but only occasionally and only on my terms.

I can't tell you when it happened, but slowly but surely, I was a little more willing to go, I even started kind of wanting to go, but I still wouldn't admit that out loud. I even listened to some of the music in secret. I still didn't buy into Jesus being my Savior, though. The people in my life who told me before that He was The Way, The Truth, and The Life, painted a much different picture through their words and actions, and if they were His people, then I didn't want anything to do with Him. Then, Recovery Church opened. My husband and the pastor there were good friends, and we had known him through A.A. prior to this, so of course, we came out to help kick it off and support him. It was there that the battle really started brewing. It had been a really long time since I had experienced the power of God coursing through a place like that.

Slowly but surely, between these two churches, things started to rattle around in my head and my heart. One day the Pastor's wife of our Sunday church told me that I should try to get off work on Sundays, and I politely said to her that I didn't feel like I needed church to be closer to my God. Now mind you, no matter how much God calls, sometimes we just blatantly don't answer. Obviously, she didn't like my answer and asked if we could get together to talk about it. So, we did. I finally told her how I truly felt and that I just wasn't sure. Her only advice was just to open the Bible. Just to start reading and seek the truth for myself. That was the best advice anyone could have given me at that time in my life. And I took it seriously. Once I was honestly open to it, God appeared to really start to pursue me. Blatantly, in my face, pursue me. I started seeking, and He met me right there. Still broken, still unclean, still unsure, and still doubting, He met me. He put all of these wonderful people and places in my life and instilled in me an earnest desire to seek the truth, to know Him.

I started going to church on Sunday more and more and never missed a Friday. I started going to Bible study at Recovery Church and got deeply plugged in. While I listened and got involved, I also cut out all of the noise, the static that didn't matter, everyone else's opinions, and flesh-fueled views. I just showed up with an open heart and mind and sought the truth. I challenged Him to show me. I needed to know for myself not through the words or stories of others but for me, and He came through clearer than ever.

One night while lying in bed, I was convicted. I knew I had reached the end of my searching and had found the one true King. I prayed, "Lord, I don't want to doubt you anymore. Show me." Jesus' face appeared clear as day behind my closed eyes, and I just cried and gave Him my life. That image is forever seared into my memory. I don't think I could ever doubt Him again if I wanted to. Sometimes my flesh doubts His will, and if He's truly for me, but in my heart of hearts, I know the truth. About a week later, still not having told a soul, I announced it at church on Sunday and man did it come as a surprise to my husband! He was already set to be baptized a week or two later, so I joined in, and together, we were baptized as followers of Jesus Christ. It was truly an awesome experience, my husband went first and then assisted the Pastor in my baptism, and I will never forget it.

Today, between our church on Sunday, Recovery Church on Friday, and the rooms of A.A., we have the most amazing support group and a life already beyond our wildest dreams. As of this year, I have started college for Drug and Alcohol counseling, we are now youth leaders at our Sunday church, and we are proud members of the leadership team at Recovery

Church Sunbury. Recovery Church has given me a place like no other to go and be open, honest, and one hundred percent myself. The joy of mixing recovery and Jesus is indescribable and has given my husband and me and so many others such joy and freedom to be able to shout the name of our Lord and Savior as loud as we can. I am honored to be a part of this movement and cannot wait to see what God has in store for this wonderful mission that is so desperately needed. I just know it will be beyond anything we could ever imagine!

Recovery has taught me how to live my life again. Jesus has shown me how to live it well. My life looks so different than it used to; I have a peace that surpasses all understanding and a zest for life (most days at least). I have rekindled a love for art and poetry, things I haven't been able to truly enjoy since before my mental health started to decline years ago. Every night I end my day by reading a devotional, gratitude journaling, and prayer. If you would have predicted my future even a year ago and told me it would be this, I would have told you that you were beyond insane and that there was no way, never, not going to happen!

As I've heard it said before, Jesus came for us, the broken, the sinners, the unwanted, the unclean, the outcasts, the lepers; He came for us and would have gladly sat at our table. He desires for us to know Him so He can heal us and send us out to show the world His grace and mercy; we just have to ask. I pray you seek Him with all of your heart. Be honest, open, and willing, and this journey will take you farther than you could ever imagine. Philippians 1:6 says, "And I am certain that God, who began the good work within you, will continue His work until it is finally finished on the day when Christ Jesus returns" (NLT). If you're reading this, He's already started something, and you can bet that He'll be faithful to finish it! I leave you with this poem I wrote, and I pray that you rely only on Him in all things:

"Oh Lord my God I'm on my knees

I've come to give thanks while the world is crushing me

Oh Lord please help me for I cannot breathe

I pray that you'll guide me, your strength is all I need

I know that you're with me through thick and through thin

You with your staff have led me from sin

You came and you found me and despite where I've been

Through your perfect love I've found home again.

Steven's Story
The Not So "Normal" Christian

My name is Steven. I am thirty-three years old, and as I write this, I am nine and half months clean and sober from alcohol and drugs, currently incarcerated for a DUI/3rd offense conviction, and walking faithfully, by His grace, with my Lord and Savior, Jesus Christ. To say my journey of faith and recovery has been a rocky and winding road would be a massive understatement. That being said, much in part to the Recovery Church Movement, I now have peace, joy, fulfillment, and so much more.

Until about the age of sixteen, I was characterized as a good kid. My parents had instilled good values. I was in the church choir, a decent student, an average athlete, and the type of young man that most parents wouldn't mind their sons and daughters associating with. Shortly after being introduced to alcohol, I became truly Dr. Jekyll and Mr. Hyde. I quickly lost interest in most hobbies, activities, school and abandoned the religion of my youth. Most relationships, both family and friends, were severed or completely lost within the first months and years of my drinking. My first detox facility was at eighteen after a tragic first semester of college which found me permanently kicked out of campus housing, suspended for nearly three weeks, and touting (all things considered) an impressive 2.0 GPA. Two short months after my first detox, my first DUI catapulted me into my first genuine attempt at recovery.

After going to inpatient treatment for three weeks, I found myself in the rooms of A.A. and was able to stay sober for nearly two and a half years due to meeting attendance and the fellowship. Looking back now, I realize that I was not actively working a program of recovery or dependent on a relationship with a higher power at any point during those two-plus years. Today I deem those two components to be essential to my sobriety. Following my relapse, after my initial sobriety, the next nearly eleven years commenced to be a wild roller coaster ride with some tremendous highs and some incredible lows. There's so much I could mention here, but I want to focus specifically on what the Lord has done in my life through the Recovery Church Movement.

Somewhere along the line, I came to the realization I needed to give God a try. After always finding myself back in the "rooms" of recovery, I kept hearing the suggestions that I needed God in my life. I tried the gods of the religion of my youth, yoga, Buddhism, meditation, and numerous other paths. When I think of myself during that time, I am reminded of the words of the apostle Paul, "Always learning and never able to come to the knowledge of the truth" (2 Timothy 3:7). In 2016, I found myself in treatment yet again. Thankfully at this treatment center, the twelve steps and developing a relationship with God were strongly encouraged. One of the staff members there who wound up being my sponsor was a believer in Jesus Christ. He invited me to church with him, and in August 2016, I truly heard the Gospel for the first time. I heard that by grace through faith, I was saved and that it was a gift from God and not dependent on my performance. Salvation. For a chronic relapser and someone who had failed repeatedly, this was really Good News.

I instantly started to crave God's Word. I was there nearly every second the doors were open. In fact, that is where I met a friend that helped disciple me and eventually introduced me to Recovery Church. I loved reading my Bible. I loved Small Group at Junior's. I love serving and kid's church. I was on fire for the things of God and was sober. However, what happened to me is I began to believe all I needed was a church. Don't hear me the wrong way. I'm not saying that Jesus is not enough because he is. However, there is such power and effectiveness afforded to the men and women that struggle with the sin problem/heart condition/disease of alcoholism and addiction through the twelve steps and working a program of recovery. I remember Junior dragging me to Recovery Church in the Bamboo Room. The vibe was truly incredible. The Spirit of God was in that place. I remember getting this amazing opportunity to ride up to Recovery Church Vero Beach with Pastor Phil and hear an incredible message about the demoniac in Mark five. I thought Recovery Church was cool, but I didn't really want to get involved. I didn't want to be an alcoholic or in recovery. I wanted Jesus to make me one of those "normal" Christians. You know, the one that looks good on Sunday morning had it all together and can maybe drink a few craft beers at a barbecue on Sunday afternoon.

It took me another few years to understand that being the "normal" Christian is not my reality. Recovery Church has been at the core of my recovery since day one of my sobriety, and it has made all the difference. Pastor Junior took me through the 12-steps and continues to sponsor and disciple me daily. There's nothing like a sponsor whose higher power is Jesus Christ. I attend Recovery Church each week. I am part of the serve team with the most incredible godly leadership at Recovery Church Delray, and I attend Lake Worth on Thursdays. My closest relationships are with people that attend and serve at Recovery Church. This movement has helped bridge the gap for me between the 12-steps fellowship and the Church.

I am no longer someone who does not want to be in recovery. I'm so grateful to be a part of the R.C. community and to tell everybody about Recovery Church. I now realize God is uniquely equipping me to witness and minister to those who have faced the same afflictions. Most recently, I've been so thankful for what I have learned through the Recovery Church Institute's Disciples Making Disciples classes. While in the Palm Beach County jail, paying the consequences for my sin and poor decisions in active addiction, I have been able to be a light in a dark place. I have been able to use many of the things I learned through R.C. to lead men to Christ and take two others through the steps. I can't wait to see my R.C. family soon and hopefully have some new attendees with me once I'm released. Eternally grateful for RCM. Your brother in Christ and recovery, Steven.

Adam's Story
The Doctor

Adam, a warrior for Jesus and Recovery, passed away at the age of 58 on August 15, 2020, following a long battle with COVID-19 pneumonia. The below testimony was recorded at Recovery Church Lake Worth a few years before his death and has been transcribed and adapted for this context. Dr. B was an influential force in the development of what was to become Recovery Church.

Welcome to Recovery Church. I got a few moments to share with you fifty-six years of a wild, strange trip. Thirty-three of those years were hell-bent on destruction, disaster, and addiction. Twenty-three years were filled with sobriety, salvation, and my savior. So, in A.A., they say we share in a general way what it was like, what happened, and what it's like now. So, I'm going to kind of do that here.

I'm not real big on drunk-a-logs or drug-a-logs; if you're sitting in a place like this listening to a moron like me, you all know how to par-tay. You don't need me to show off and show that I did it like this; I did it like that, I did it with a wiffle ball bat. We all know how to get down, and we all know how to get dirty, and some of us have stayed that way for a long time, okay, and I was one of those people.

In case you misunderstand what I'm going to say, I'm not saying any of this to blame or name someone. I'm just giving you an idea of what set my psyche into motion. I'm from Rhode Island. Go Pats. I was brought up in a small town called Smithfield, and I was born into a very, very, let's just say, dysfunctional family. I had a shameless, perfectionistic, rageaholic, abusive father and an alcoholic, codependent, suicidal mother.

I was the first child born into that meat grinder. I adopted the unspoken role that I had to make all things right. I had to fix this thing; I believed this thing was all messed up because of me, so I had to do something to fix this. This was the life growing up. Until I went to college away from that nonsense.

So, I heard from my father that "You're no good," "You'll be on skid row without a red cent," "You're a product of a whore, the best part of you ran down my leg." And all sorts of other loving things that every child growing up should hear from his father. My father never came to any of my sporting events; he never did any of the father-son stuff. Surely never told me or showed me he loved me, and he just kept telling me I was no good, and my mother was no good.

He used a lot of words that I can't use here. But some of you came from that side of the neighborhood; you know what I'm talking about. The dynamic I had going on inside of me was "you're no good, you're no good, you're no good", and I kept responding, "no I am, no I am, that's not true; that's a lie." But there was something going on I didn't understand. Although in my head, I understood the concept that my father was whacked and what he was saying wasn't true about my mother and me. I loved my mother, even though we had to find her vodka, pour half out, and water it down so she wouldn't drink too much and overdose. We had to take her valiums and switch them with pills that looked like valiums, so she wouldn't be successful at committing suicide. But still, there was this dynamic going on inside of me in my head that I knew was wrong.

If you hear day in and day out, you're no good. No matter what you're saying to yourself in your head, your heart begins to reflect that message your father gave you. And so even though I thought I was this, and I was supposed to be that, I was doing this, and I was that.... etc., deep inside, I was never good enough. And so, when I became old enough, somewhere in my teens, to not want to be part of that anymore, I kind of divorced myself from that. I resigned myself to the fact I was not going to have a father.

So, I decided I would have to be my own father. And the real problem with that was since I was going to be my own father, I only had one example to go by. So, I thought my father was abusive; you should have seen how I took over and what I ended up doing to myself for a whole lot of years. My life became, basically a suicide run without the intention of suicide. That was the dynamic that got the ball rolling.

I became on the outside, a human doing instead of a human being. My dynamic was that if I could just be good enough, my father would accept me, love me, and give me what I needed. And so, when it came to school, I thought if I just brought home good grades, they would respect me, they would love me, they would change, and they'd love each other. If I'm just good enough, my mother wouldn't want to kill herself, wouldn't be drinking. I became this overzealous human doing. I brought home the highest grades that the town ever saw. I was the high school's valedictorian, the captain of all the teams, and I set records and did all this stuff. My father still never came to any of it. He wouldn't even sign my report card, even though all the grades on it were hundreds. From that point on, I realized no matter what I did, it wasn't going to be good enough.

Of course, you learn along that journey in a small town they have booze, and they have pot, and they have cigarettes, and if you're really lucky, you get mushrooms and mescaline once in a while and you had to go downtown in the metro to go get the white stuff, and you had to have some money. So basically, I drank if you left some unattended, and I would smoke your dope for you to help you out. You could have the cigarette. I'm playing sports. I am not going to do that. But I want to do the other stuff full-on, and that kind of began a real love affair. Because when I took that drink and I smoked that dope, something happened, that big black pit, a burning misery inside of me, the pain from that hole inside my chest went away for a while. Then I could be cool and instead of being all fear-based anxious and self-conscious and shy, I could be loose and cool. It was a social lubricant. This was something like Bill Wilson's story in the *Big Book* of A.A. He talked about how alcohol was this alloy that was later going to be boomeranged back and eventually come back and hit him in the head. That's what was going to happen to me. For a long time, alcohol and drugs were a constant friendly companion, so they went with me to college.

Yes, I had to work three jobs through college. It was an Ivy League school, and it was pretty damn expensive. And so, I borrowed as much money as I could, the maximum amount of loans. I worked three jobs and I got myself through undergrad. I got accepted to medical school. The United States military was at the same time having a shortage of doctors and other professionals, so they developed this thing called the HPSP, and they would pay for your medical school, provided you put a year of service in for every year they pay. So, I go up to the fool with the fancy uniform, and I say, "You tell me you're going to pay for my medical school?" He says, "Yes, we are." "You're going to pay for my medical school, and you're going to allow me to come into the service and work? Do you mean like these college loans? I am not going to have to pay until I'm 40 years old anymore?" That was the ticket for me to go to medical school.

I was from a broken home, so I was in a lot of broken relationships. I had another addiction going on called sex and love addiction, codependency. It's called by a lot of names. I had modeled for me very unhealthy relationships. When I would be out there trying to get myself a honey, all of a sudden, when I put my eyes on one particular one, my heart would go boom, boom, boom, boom and you see I thought that was chemistry, I thought she was the one for me. But I didn't know that it was chemistry that inside me it was a warning system that said, "No! No! She's got a gun. Get out of there. She's going to kill you! Run!"

I went to the very one that was going to do me the most harm, and I had one busted relationship, one busted heart, one busted situation after another. You think you'd learn after a while. Hey, last time it turned out bad; I don't want to do that again. Well codependency is progressive, just like alcoholism.

Every single relationship I got into got worse, even though I thought I was learning, oh man, I'm not going to get into that again, I'm going to get me a fine woman next time, and suddenly, boom, I'm in a deeper part than before. And this happened over and over and over.

I ended up marrying a real off the hook one. She was going to take me hostage, and she was going to fix me. I wasn't going to have anything to do with it, and she had this little secret among others. One secret was that her family had this birth defect running through generations. So much so that the United States navy had studied her family and studied the genes of the kidney and hearing and all this other stuff. I get married, and we have a son while in my anesthesiology residency. My son was born with the same birth defects. In fact, I had to perform the resuscitation when he was born. While my son was being born, let's just say, I had to leave the head of the table, and I went to the foot of the table, and catch the package. I had to bring him over to the bassinet, perform the resuscitation, call the NICU, and begin the fun and games that ended up with about a dozen surgeries for the first year of his life. My hope vanished of being able to raise the victory over my childhood by having a son, be the coach and supportive father that I never had. That moment in that hospital at that bassinet, I realized, you know what, that wasn't going to happen. I began to sink into a resentment so deep and so dark that I'm surprised I'm alive to tell you about it today. Because as an anesthesiology resident at the third busiest surgical hospital in the country, I performed about seven hundred surgical procedures a year. I had my hands on one boatload of operating room grade fentanyl, not the watered down with that cotton candy heroin stuff you see on the streets, but straight fentanyl.

I was a first-year junior resident. A senior resident by the name of Dave had also the same appetite for such a substance. One day during my first year, there was a big commotion in the hospital because that fool was found dead in the cold room with a needle in his arm. When I went through the pain of that birth of my son, I had the thought that "Boy, that stuff must have made you feel real good. If that guy Dave was willing to take it and die using it, I think that just maybe that stuff is going to help me feel better." I slipped that needle into my vein, and I started to realize, unbeknownst to me at the beginning, of course, that it was a short-acting, very powerful synthetic opiate that is extremely addicting. I got addicted, and I went on a dark road, not caring whether I was going to live or die.

I believe it was divine intervention that kept me from dying. I was intervened on because when you're shooting a boatload of fentanyl, you're not eating that much, you're not feeling too good because of the constant withdrawal, you're losing weight, and you've got dark circles under your eyes. People are going to take notice of that when you come to work sweating early every morning in withdrawal. So luckily, people noticed and cared enough about me to get me some help. I ended up having a whole bunch of powers intervening and namely the Connecticut Board of Medicine. They put their thumb on me for a while. I did what I was supposed to do when I was supposed to do it. I was the first and only resident ever to be readmitted with a fentanyl addiction back to Hartford hospital. I completed my residency by repeating my last year.

I got on that highway after my residency, drove as far south as I-95 went, and got my first job as a staff anesthesiologist. In three and a half years after my first round of recovery, after working a little over a year at JFK, there were a whole lot of changes in medicine. I didn't know and didn't learn through that first round of recovery that not only was this disease cunning and powerful, but it was also patient and insidious. Some of you people might know that it was the evolution of managed care, and there were things called HMOs. They started to really pinch the hospital-based physicians like pathologists, audiologists, anesthesiologists. All those promises and all those things that are in my contract, as far as being a partner and getting that hundred thousand dollar raise all went out the window. One day, I started to develop that resentment again, and I thought to myself, "Well, I'm going to do all the work, and I'm not going to get all the pay. Well, I surely deserve something. I'll tell you what. They got a whole lot of fentanyl in this place too. Maybe I want to get high if I'm going to be all locked up in this joint. I might as well enjoy it." So, I took me a whole bunch of that. I went to the bathroom and began a several months journey this time, instead of years like before.

I forgot this disease was progressive. In less than two months, I was taking four times the amount of fentanyl I was taking during my first two-year run. I was taking 120 CCs a day, and if you've ever had the operating room stuff, the big bottles come in 20 CC bottles. So 120 CCs or six of those bottles is four times the amount to put somebody into a coma for cardiac bypass surgery. I was taking that every day, walking around doing my job as a doctor. But was I really living? No, I was dying. I got intervened. There weren't all nice people to help me this time. People in the hospital said, "Get out of here Holmes. You must be so messed up to do that. If something happens, we're getting sued." So, they just basically kicked me out. If you ever go from taking 120 CCs a day of fentanyl to none, something's going to happen to you.

I spent four days in a bathtub, stuff coming out of every end. I got in the tub, like one last great act of nobility, because I really thought I was going to die. I was convinced there's no way I'm going to survive. I wanted to die. There's a lot of mess happening as I'm dying. I thought to myself when my family comes in and finds me it'll be much easier to clean up the corpse and mess if it's all in the tub and can wash down the drain. I figured I was doing a great thing, so I hung out in the tub and waited. I'm wanting to die. I'm wishing to die, but days are going by, and I'm not dying.

Three, maybe four days later. I'm not only not dying, but

I'm feeling a little bit better. I might even be able to get up out of that tub. I let the water run on me because it wasn't a pretty sight. I got out of that tub. Now that I realized I wasn't going to die, I was like, oh man, I got to go check my cell phone out, to see what's going on. There had been a bunch of people calling, trying to get me into treatment. Long story short, when I kind of got myself together, I drove down to this place in South Florida. Let me tell you something, I was absolutely livid because my best friend, my lover, my comforter, my strength, my courage, my helper had turned against me, and bit a hole in my entire life.

While driving into that facility, I got an idea of what I was going to go through because I've been through this treatment thing before. My attitude was a whole bunch different. As the first-time treatment was happening to me, I was like, "Oh my, what is this?" Then this time going to treatment, it didn't happen to me, it happened for me. I was going to go there no matter what they told me to do; I was going to do it because let me tell you one thing, I was never, listen to me, I was never going to ever feel like that and go through that four-day hell ever again. If they told me, "Hey fatty, get your butt over there and put your nose on the floor and get on your hands and knees", I wouldn't ask no questions; I'd be diving on the floor. Whatever they told me to do, I took note of it, and it became a life and death effort. When I got out, I got me to an A.A. meeting at the Easy Does It Club's six o'clock, and that became my home group The Happy Hour, Monday, and Friday. They had both a smoking room and a small non-smoking room. On Tuesday at six o'clock, there was a meeting called the Good Guys. So, I was going Monday, Tuesday, and Friday to this six o'clock meeting.

I got me a sponsor. I didn't even trust my own picking because you know how I picked women. If I were going to pick a sponsor, I wouldn't do so good with that. So, I went over this guy I saw at every meeting. His name was Jack. "Jack, you know me, I'm a little bit twisted in the brain stem here, you know, a little insane in the membrane. I probably need a real good sponsor. I don't really trust my own thinking; I don't want to pick a sponsor. But if you were me or were kind of coaching me, do you know who would be able to handle a nut job like me?" He says, "Oh yes, you are one whack case, bro. You need a lot of help. You need a tough guy. You need a guy who's not going to take your crap. I know, you need a guy by the name of Phil, or maybe Tom, or maybe Russell." I look over and say "You mean that Russell?" He goes, "Yeah, that Russell."

Russel was talking to some guy, so I did what any Italian would do, I pushed that other guy out of the way, and I introduced myself to Russell. "Jack over there is saying you want to sponsor me, I need some help, can you help me?" And so, he smiled this real, you know what I'm talking about when I say a real smile? See, I had this fake smile on for thirty-three years, dying inside, wanting to be cool, wanting to be smooth, wanting to be accepted... but this guy had a gleam, the sparkle, this twinkle in his eye and he had this real peace smile going on. When I saw that, I was like, "I need that." He did something crazy, he handed me his business card and he says, "If you're serious about me sponsoring you, call me every day," and he did something that normally would have got the fool killed. He pushed me out of the way. He said, "I'm talking to this guy." Doesn't he know who I think I am? What is going on here? So, I had me a sponsor, and I went over to that guy's house every Wednesday at six o'clock for about seven-plus months.

I can't tell you much about what we did, he gave me writing assignments, I wrote all this stuff and had no idea what I was doing. But I did what he said, and I went over to his house. I was in five minutes early, and we sat there, and we worked. The only thing I remember from that time was that when I walked out of his house about an hour and a half later, I felt better than when I was walking into his house, and I couldn't explain that. It wasn't like he was smoking dope and giving me some, you know what I'm saying. We're just reading out of the *Big Book* and writing stuff. But somehow, I had all this hate, I wanted to kill him, for giving me all that crap work, and I was going to punch him in the face, but he'd open that door, and there was that smile again, and I was like damn, that smile got me. I did this work, walked out of the house, and didn't want to kill my sponsor. I was actually caring about what he was saying and trusted him. This thing started to happen for me in the steps, and then one day, he turned me loose on sponsoring some other people. I started working with people, the stuff in the book began to come alive. It was not just for the guy I was working with, but it started coming alive for me.

The thing that rocked my world was one day working with a guy on step six. I realized that part of the *Big Book* on page 53 where it says, "God is either everything or God is nothing. God either is, or he isn't. What's our choice to be?" And at that point, I realized this thing you were talking about, I just thought it was some fancy, funny, hocus-pocus thing to make us all not kill each other, but it was real. You mean there's this all-powerful, all-intelligent creator of the universe, and he's actually interested in a puke like me? And he's not only interested in a puke like me. He's allowing me to help a puke like this sitting next to me. Man, I want to know a God like that better because I've done a lot of really bad stuff in my life. But despite all that, there is a God who loves me, and there is a God who forgives me, and there is a God who restores me, and there is a God who wants to have a relationship with me, and there is a God who wants to walk with me. And there is a God who wants to show more of himself to me, and there is a God who wants to display all the love and all the power and all the good stuff that he can do in this life, in and for and through me. And for twenty-three years, this has been my story. And for twenty-three years, I haven't had to pick up another white chip. I had the blessing of taking more than a hundred men through the 12-steps of alcohol anonymous. I get to watch their lives change, watch them sponsor people who sponsor people. They've helped me more than what little I could give to help them.

This whole process was showing me the plan God had for my life. You see, God's plan for my life wasn't for me to drink and drug myself into an early grave. God wants me to have life abundantly and to spend an eternity of perfection with him, avoiding the deep fires of a place without. If you're alive today, and you're not dead by your addiction, I want to offer you this idea: Whether you knew God, whether you know God, whether you believe in God, whether you accept God or not, God is believing in you, and God is accepting you, and God is helping you, and God is saving you, even when you were trying to kill yourself. A God like that is worth getting to know a lot better and by as direct means as possible. Thanks for letting me share.

Junior's Story
The Rejected Child

My name is Junior, and by the Grace of God, on March 28th, 2022, I celebrated nine years (including nights and weekends) free from drugs and alcohol. I never thought it possible to stay sober and not have a desire for drugs and alcohol, but I quickly found out that with God, "all things are possible." Today, I am free from the desire to use drugs or alcohol, and I know that God did it. So how did I get here? Well, that's a question I asked one too many times in my life.

At a young age, I wanted to be successful. Being raised by a single mom who did her best to raise five kids, I always wanted to be successful and experience the finer things in life. At that time, I actually had something very powerful that I didn't know I had. I had Hope. Hope that one day life would be better. No matter what was going on in my life, I could always dream of the day that I became successful and got to enjoy what I thought were the finer things in life. It wasn't easy growing up, but hope helped.

My dad left before I was born because he didn't want to have another kid, and that kid he didn't want to have, was me. I felt rejected by the father I had never met. Years later, my stepfather, who I considered my dad, also left. I felt rejected by my stepfather. By the time I got to High School, I had begun to see a pattern of being left and started to feel like maybe I was unlovable. I started believing that lie, and even I didn't love me. I guess you could say I was on their side and made-up reasons why we all shouldn't love me. I was really shy in high school. I saw myself like Steve Urkel from the show Family Matters. I felt like I annoyed everyone, and no one wanted to be around me. But see, Steve Urkel was a scientist and had created this fancy machine that when he stepped into it, he would come out as Stephan Urkelle. Stephan was cool. He was the guy everyone wanted to be. Oh, how I wish I could have been Stephan

Urkelle, but I wasn't smart enough to build that machine, so I was stuck being Junior. I hated being Junior.

I remember being in high school and wanting so badly to be accepted, but I told myself that no one would like me; heck, I didn't even like me. For the first time, I understood why people joined gangs. They just wanted to belong. I was desperate to be liked and was willing to do whatever it took to be accepted. So the first time someone invited me to drink alcohol, I knew it was wrong, but for once, I was invited, and it felt good to be wanted. So I took that drink, and I got to tell you, I understood why they called alcohol liquid courage. I looked like Junior, but I felt like Stephan, and the feeling was good enough for me. I had found my answer. Alcohol became my new friend. I ran to alcohol whenever I was angry, sad, happy, lonely, or anxious, and it became my answer.

So, I graduated high school and made it to the real world. The only problem was that even though I had the grades, I couldn't attend college because I wasn't legally in the United States. That was depressing. The college experience looked so amazing on TV. Oh well, I would never experience it, call it Junior luck again, but the good news is that my friend alcohol would comfort me. At this point in my life, alcohol invited someone of its friends to the party called "illegal drugs," and they became my answer as well. Alcohol and drugs brought me comfort, but what I didn't know was what I turned to for comfort in one season would become my prison in the next.

I met these business guys who took a liking to me and taught me how to trade commodities and make money. I became really good at selling and acquiring "stuff," all the stuff I had dreamed of when I was a kid. The things I thought would make me happy, only to find out none of them brought the joy I thought they would bring. They brought short-term happiness followed by emptiness. At 29 years old, having everything I thought I wanted, I fell into depression with suicidal thoughts. I hated life, it had no meaning or purpose, and I no longer wanted to live. To top it off, I was addicted to drugs and alcohol and couldn't shake the habit. I tried going from liquor to beer, beer to wine, wine to smoking weed, only to realize I would be more addicted to all of them.

On March 27th, 2013, I asked God to take my life. I didn't have a relationship with God, but I knew there was a God. As I prayed that prayer, I thought about the definition of insanity. "Doing the same thing over and over and expecting different results." So, I decided to do one thing differently. The next day, I would Google "I have a problem with alcohol" and try to get help. I knew nothing about A.A, the 12-steps, recovery, or treatment, but the next day as I searched for help, I stumbled upon a treatment center whose slogan was "We Restore Hope," and it dawned on me…that's what I lost, Hope. I no longer had hope in anything or anyone. I realized clinical depression can be described as seeing no light at the end of the tunnel. When all hope seems gone, depression can set in.

I went to that treatment center, and for the first time in years, I was able to have a few days without drugs or alcohol in my body. It was refreshing. They had an optional morning Christian devotional time, and I decided to join. I loved it. It had been years since I had been to church because church people judged me, and I didn't want to be in an environment where I wasn't wanted. But church, in a treatment center, that was different. I truly felt like I could come as I am, and no one would judge me, and if they did judge me, I had a good come back, "You're in here too."

After a few weeks of being in treatment, they allow you to leave the property, but the only option was to go to church. I remember sitting with a guy from the Christian devotional meeting, and he said, "Hey man, let's go to church today. You're at two weeks. You can finally leave property", and I replied, "No, I'm not going to church, God doesn't want anything to do with me." He insisted and said, "Come on, man, you'll like church." I replied, "Let me clean myself up first and get my act together, then I'll go to church." The sad thing is, I really thought I needed to get clean first and be righteous before I could show up in the "House of the Lord." Looking back now, I realize it's like saying, "Let me get fit first, then I'll go to the gym!" You don't get fit, then go to the gym; you go to the gym to get fit. He asked one more time, and I replied, "Don't ask me again. I'm not going" then, as he walked away, he said, "Well, there's real coffee at church," to which I replied, "Real coffee? You know what, I've been wanting to go to church. Let's do it!" This treatment center only had decaf coffee, and I would have done anything for a real cup of coffee at that point.

I remember arriving at a fancy church in downtown West Palm Beach, FL. All of us addicts were hopping out of this big white van we call "the druggy buggy." I remember stepping out, and we all sparked up cigarettes. Most of us had tattoos except for me. I remember thinking to myself, "We look bad as a unit. People are probably judging us right now; we totally look like addicts". As I walked into that church, I had to deal with all this negative self-talk of how we looked bad and how everyone was judging us. I had been judged before at church, so the enemy knew right where to poke.

As the pastor was preaching the sermon, I couldn't receive anything he was saying because I was so stuck in my head with all this negative self-talk. After a while, I prayed and pleaded with God to give me a moment of clarity so I could hear the message, and God did. It was that day that I heard the story of the prodigal son, and I sensed God saying, "Son, I'm not your accuser. I'm your defender. Just like the adulterous woman in John Chapter 8, I fight for you when everyone else wants to call you guilty. I am your advocate. Stop running from me and start running to me". That day my whole world changed. I started seeing God in a new light. I started seeing God for who He really was instead of the religious condemning God that I had inherited from. That day, I experienced God's love, Grace, and Mercy. I decided to surrender my life, and my life has never been the same.

I moved into a halfway house and lived there for a year, got a sponsor, went to A.A. meetings every day, got plugged into a church, and started serving there. I joined a small group, read my Bible, spent time with God daily, and surrounded myself with great God-loving people. Anything I was asked to do, I did it, and for some reason, taking suggestions from the right people produced the right results. Life was amazing.

After a while, I was getting tired of A.A. meetings and told my therapist I was no longer doing A.A. I would only go to Church moving forward as I felt like "recovery people" complained a lot, and Church people, no matter what they were going through, had hope in God, and I wanted to be around hopefully positive people. I quickly found out I needed both. Church people helped me grow closer to God and in a deeper understanding of the Bible, but they knew nothing about my recovery. They would ask me questions like, "Why can't you drink?" "Aren't you a new creation? and Jesus's first miracle was to turn water into wine." Dangerous question to be asking a newly sober addict. My "recovery friends" taught me how to answer that question. They reminded me that I was allergic to alcohol and when I drank, I broke out in handcuffs. The Big Book of A.A. says, "One drink is too much, and a thousand is never enough." I totally agree with that statement. Prior to this time of getting sober, after three months of success, I believed someone who told me I could drink like a gentleman, and for the next year and a half, I was intoxicated and using drugs daily. I will stick to what the Big Book says about this malady.

So, I attended Church in addition to A.A. but always dreamed of having a church for addicts and alcoholics. A place where we can talk about Jesus freely and about our addiction without feeling judged or condemned. The church I was a part of had a recovery ministry, and I enjoyed it, but over time, I saw that all the alcoholics and drug addicts were leaving, and it became a place where the pastors would send anyone with any hurt, habit, or hang up. So, we had a lot of codependents, overeaters, sex addicts, and even lonely people join. There is nothing wrong with that. The program just seemed to move away from helping addicts and alcoholics as their focus. So, the people from A.A. that I would invite all seemed to leave.

Over time, our leaders imploded. We replaced them with new leaders, and they also imploded, so we shut down our recovery ministry. The pastors of the church asked me, and another young lady named Christine to start a recovery ministry geared towards helping drug addicts and alcoholics. As we began to dream of what that would look like, we suggested, "what if we were to create a Sunday morning type of experience at night and gear the message towards addicts? We would have two to three worship songs, a message from the Bible geared towards addicts, and then a time of open share where people can talk about what they are walking through." We all liked the idea and started working towards creating it.

That week, someone asked us if we had ever heard of Recovery Church. "Recovery Church, what's that?" I asked. They gave us the info, and we decided to check it out. I remember pulling up and seeing hundreds of addicts and alcoholics gathered together, grabbing coffee. Then, a worship band came out and started playing familiar worship music. It was amazing. You could feel the Holy Spirit flowing through the room. Next, someone came out to make announcements, and then a pastor started teaching from the Bible but used a lot of "recovery" language. I had never seen that done before. This was almost exactly what we dreamed of. Then after the message, they asked us to take a 10-minute break and come back for an open share. OK, now this was exactly what we dreamed of, and it was even better than we had imagined.

Christine came to me that night and said, "Junior, I have good news and bad news!" I replied, "What's the good news?" She said, "This place is amazing, and I love it." Then I asked, "What's the bad news?" She said, "I no longer feel called to start a recovery ministry at our church. I feel called to serve at Recovery Church!" I replied, "I totally understand. You have to follow where God leads."

The next day, I had a meeting with the Pastors, and they asked, "Junior, how was it last night?" I replied, "Awesome, but I have good news and bad news." They asked, "What's the good news?" I replied, "Recovery Church is legit and exactly what we have been dreaming of." They asked, "So what's the bad news?" I replied, "Christine loves it so much that she feels called to serve there. So, she will not be building another one here." We started serving at Recovery Church and loved it. We never did create the recovery ministry at our home church. We figured, if someone down the street from us is already doing it well, why reinvent the wheel? Let's partner with them and start making an impact for the Kingdom together, and so we did.

About a year later, God called me to move up to Charlotte, NC, to a ministry training program to become a Pastor. I thought I moved up to Charlotte to learn ministry, but looking back, God brought me to Charlotte so I could meet my beautiful/amazing wife, Amanda. It turns out ministry was just a plus. I got to be part of Elevation Church for a season and was assigned to two different campuses UC & Matthews. My time there was incredible, and I learned so much about ministry.

In January 2018, God called me back to Florida to be a Pastor at my home church. It was such an honor to come back to the team and people that helped shape me and now be part of giving back to that community. My wife helped me realize the reason God called me back to FL was for Recovery Church. We had nothing like it in Charlotte, and she knew I loved working with addicts and alcoholics. As soon as I returned, I quickly jumped back into serving at Recovery Church. We saw God do amazing things. Hundreds were finding freedom from drug and alcohol addiction and were getting saved. Recovery Church began to grow nationwide, and God was up to something great.

April 2021, my wife, and I took a leap of faith to join Recovery Church full time. We were nervous but truly sensed God was calling us to make this move. It was the best decision we could have made. GOD has done some amazing things in and through Recovery Church in the past few years, and we believe the best is yet to come. We have faith God is going to put a Recovery Church in every city in America and beyond because too many people are dying without knowing Jesus.

This year, I got to celebrate nine years of sobriety. God has blessed me with a wonderful wife, two beautiful boys, JR and Avery, a house, community, I get to work with Pastor Phil Dvorak, one of the humblest leaders you will ever meet, and I get to serve in my dream job. I once heard it said, "Find what you love to do, and you'll never have to work another day in your life." I find that statement to be true. I aspire to inspire until I expire and pray to help others find purpose so they can live purposeful lives and never have to work another day in their life. May God bless you.

Janice's Story
The Lost Soul

My name is Janice, and I am an alcoholic and a believer in Jesus Christ. My sober date is December 5th, 2017.

I was born to two alcoholic parents on August 9th, 1960. When I was five, my parents divorced, and my dad's family also divorced me. I never saw them again. Alcoholism seemed to be in my blood. My father's side of the family all drank. On my mother's side, only my mother drank. At a very young age, I felt abandoned and unloved.

At the age of twelve, I was pretty much in charge of the household. My mother told my sister and me if we wanted to smoke weed or drink, to do it in the house. She did not want the police to bring us home. My drinking career continued until I was thirty-one years old. I was trying to fill that empty hole in my heart of being unloved and abandoned with alcohol and many failed relationships. I wanted to be loved so bad it didn't matter if my relationships were with males or females.

I was a dry drunk for twenty-two years until my partner of twenty years passed away. I was so tired of taking care of people. "The party was on." Oh, this party lasted until I lost everything, got two DUIs, and went to jail and rehab.

I started going to meetings, found a sponsor, and worked the Steps. Some friends of mine from AA brought me to church one Sunday, where I received a Bible. Funny thing, I never picked up a Bible until I was fifty-nine years old. What the heck was I waiting for? Then, I was taken to a place called Recovery Church, and that was it. I have been going there for three years. I became a believer in Jesus Christ and eventually got baptized.

On December 5th, 2022, I will have five years sober. I currently have my own home, and I have a job. I have an awesome community of sober friends who have become my family. I am a faithful servant of God. I am blessed to be able to help other alcoholics, addicts, and others in need. None of this would have been possible without God, all my sober community, and prayers.

Mitch's Story
The Small-Town Kid

I grew up in North Central, Iowa, in a very small rural town, and I am one of three children. My childhood was good, and I have very fond memories. I was a very active kid and participated in many sports. My parents were owner/operators of restaurants, and they worked very long hours. So, I didn't always spend a lot of time with them. But I have fond memories of my parents and my home life growing up. They always made us feel special and loved.

When I was about eleven, my mom told us that she was going to leave for thirty days to receive treatment for alcohol. I had never seen her drink, but obviously, there was an issue. She explained how she had spiraled very quickly out of control drinking during the past few months. With the financial assistance of a godly man in our small town, my mother went to a treatment center in Texas for thirty days, returned to Iowa, and never had another drink. Praise Be to God! Through my mom alcohol affected me in very personal way at a young age. Both my grandfathers died as a direct or indirect result of alcohol. I also have several uncles, cousins, and a brother that have fought and continue to fight addictions.

My immediate family growing up, was not Christian at all. We never attended church, although I did attend Sunday School as a young child for a year or so, but I don't remember even believing or thinking about God. Today though, I can look back and see how God was often planting seeds in my childhood and life that just took a little while to bear fruit. I am so incredibly thankful for his patience, unrelenting love, and pursuit of my heart!

My drinking started at a very young age. My first drink was around the age of thirteen, and although I don't remember much about that night, it was the start of an addiction that would bring me years of pain and suffering. Shortly after my introduction to alcohol, I started to attend parties and drink with friends. Almost immediately, consequences came into play, such as citations for underage possession of alcohol and public urination, not to mention the amount of brain cells and money wasted. I also was not allowed to compete on my high school wrestling team my junior year because I was caught at a party.

I was on to college, where my drinking took off. Now I had the freedom to drink when I wanted with no parental oversight. It was in college that I started to experiment with drugs. I quickly started smoking marijuana pretty much daily and experimenting with a variety of other drugs. I was a binge drinker then, as I would be for the next ten to twelve years. I would drink hard and fast and always for the purpose of getting drunk. I loved the feeling of getting drunk. This time in my life, I started having blackouts quite frequently. But, because I surrounded myself with people just like me, "I never had a problem."

I was always decently popular and had many friends, but somehow still felt alone and insecure. This insecurity always went away when I drank, and I was able to be the fun-loving guy who wasn't afraid of speaking to anyone. Alcohol helped me be the guy I thought I wanted to be. I would say and do crazy things in my drunkenness, and upon sobering up, these escapades would bring on great shame, which further fueled the insecurity and the addiction. People would tell me the crazy things I did and said, and I remember how badly I hated the thought of being that person...And yet I continued to drink... "Cunning and baffling," no doubt.

The scary part about my addiction was that I was able to binge drink and therefore was a functional alcoholic for many years. I had no problem attending class and work. Never really giving all of me to anything but partying. Because of my ability to work and still function, my addiction stayed somewhat hidden and relatively non-destructive (at least outwardly) for almost twenty years. Inwardly I was killing myself and ruining any chance of genuine relationships. I didn't have many real friends and was more and more alienating myself from family.

Alcohol and partying are what brought me to Florida. I graduated from college and thought, what better place to continue the party. A good friend and I moved to West Palm Beach and continued to party like before. About five years after moving to Florida, I started to think that maybe there was an issue with my drinking and started to attend A.A. meetings sporadically and vowing almost weekly to my friends and co-workers that I was going to quit drinking. My repeated failures and ongoing pledges to quit became a laughing matter to those around me... "Mitch is quitting drinking again!" Out of "self-will," I would stay sober for four weeks or maybe six. But, more often than not, I would quit long enough (three-four days) for my head to clear and for my body to start feeling normal again. I was unwilling to do any twelve-step work and couldn't stop drinking. I remember going to Barnes and Noble and looking in the self-help section for the cure to stop drinking. I bought that day a book about "the easy way to quit drinking." Guess what? It didn't work for me. I have heard that "comfort is a killer." It almost took me out.

Then July 7th, 2007, I was arrested in Delray Beach for felony possession of cocaine just steps away from the church that would ultimately help me to help start Recovery Church Delray Beach. This was it!! I was done!! Catastrophic! I remember sitting in jail thinking I am done. But, as you may relate, this wasn't enough. After my stint in jail, I chose to enter the Drug Court Program of Palm Beach County. Whereupon successful completion, my felony charge could be expunged. In that program, though, I still drank and used cocaine. I completed this program by God's grace and successfully expunged my felony.

Part of the requirements for the drug court program was attending A.A. meetings. It was through attending these court-ordered meetings I connected with a godly man who sponsored me. God had given me the willingness at that point to say I was powerless over drugs and alcohol and I needed him to help me recover. Up to this point, I had never believed in or wanted anything to do with God! In high school, I remember ridiculing my sister about believing in God and claiming that no God exists. I remember latching on to the slogan "Religion was for the weak-minded," whom I heard from an incredibly intelligent man Jessie "the Body" Ventura. You know, the professional wrestler turned governor of Minnesota. LOL.

My sponsor started opening my eyes to Jesus and showing me His handiwork all around me. He then introduced me to Church and the Bible, and very quickly, I found myself answering an altar call at Calvary Chapel Boynton Beach. In God's providential plan for me, my sponsor and I decided to open a Christian halfway house. The blessings I received because of my involvement and management of this ministry are too many to count! God did a great work in me and dozens of other men who today are sober and seeking Jesus because of that ministry.

Jesus began a good work in me despite my best efforts to push him away! Slowly he started to change me and mold me into who he wanted me to be. Working through my steps brought me incredible freedom. What I found from doing my steps was that I was incredibly selfish and incredibly insecure. Both of which kept me drinking and drugging for many years! God, in His faithfulness, has chiseled away some of that insecurity and selfishness through many years of discipleship and 12-step work. Jesus died on the cross so that I could be free from shame and guilt, and I no longer need others' approval because I have the approval of the ONE who really matters! God has radically changed me and my thought process, and I am forever grateful!

Through my sobriety and relationship with the Lord, he gave me the greatest blessing in my family! God had so radically renewed my mind that I was able to commit to one woman for a lifetime. In His incredible love for me, he placed not just any woman in my life but a Godly woman, and He sat her next to me at church! I never thought I could commit to one woman and date one in a Godly manner. But, by His power, I was able to glorify Him in our relationship, and we remained celibate throughout our dating! Jolene showed me grace like I had never received before. Then God decided to bless us with two beautiful and amazing sons. Once upon a time, because of my addiction, I relinquished to the thought that I would never have children.

A few short years after getting sober, I was called into leadership and then full-time vocational ministry at The Avenue Church. I would have never dreamed of working in a church. At The Avenue Church, I really matured in Christ because of the time and love of mature men in Christ pouring into me. Through the church, God called me to serve as a chaplain for the Delray Beach Police Department, which was the same department that arrested me!

During the beginning of the COVID-19 pandemic back in June 2020, we chose to launch RC Delray, and we have never looked back. God raised up an army of servant leaders who have freely given of themselves to help others find Jesus and sobriety! We have seen God move so mightily at Recovery Church Delray Beach, and we are currently building a team to launch another Recovery Church in South Florida.

Today I get to serve as an employee of The Recovery Church Movement. Only God could author a story so beautiful. The gratitude I feel for His call and love upon my life is priceless, and today I get to be used by Him to help others find Him and recovery!

Billy's Story
The Restless Man

As a child, I never imagined myself being so defeated. I remember the early years when everything seemed so perfect. From the outside, life appeared to be normal. I enjoyed school, had lots of friends, and played sports. It was just the way it was supposed to be. I was loved at home and looked forward to life.

When I looked back over my addiction, I learned I was, in more ways than one, prepped from an early age to become an addict. Addiction truly is the symptom of a much deeper problem. As a child, I went to Catholic school and had a very basic understanding of God. As a kid, who needed any more than that? At the age of nine, something happened to me that profoundly changed me. I felt real fear for the first time. I was sexually abused by a neighbor girl. I knew it was wrong, but there was a part of me that wanted it to feel right. Walking out of the house, I felt this overwhelming guilt and shame. Deep down, I knew something was wrong. I was raised differently. This was something I could not make right. What was done was done. There was no going back to the old child. I lived in fear every day that I had contracted a disease. I had this feeling God was not happy with me. I believed I was dirty and marred, never to be clean again.

I did not know how to process what happened to me, nor did I feel comfortable talking about it. What would my family think? I was isolated and scared. I thought maybe I could pretend everything was fine and go back to the way it was. That was not possible. Every time I drove past the house, I was reminded of what had happened. I would hold my breath for the entire block. I recall sitting in our Christmas Eve service that year and breaking into tears. I felt so guilty and broken. I did not like this feeling of being alone. My parents did not know how to respond. I am not positive I clearly communicated what happened, but just enough

153

to get it off my chest. What could they do? There was no solution. I could not go back to the child I was before.

My youth was troubled from that point on. I did things to feel accepted. I was looking for attention. I remember Children and Youth Services getting involved. I was not a bad kid; I just needed some extra attention. They assigned a type of big brother/case worker to me. His name was Joe. I remember Joe was like the friend I never had. I really looked up to him. He was easy to talk to. I do not recall things changing much, but I do remember having a safe place to be me with no masks on. Joe would also counsel my parents, trying to help them understand and raise me. I had a troubled older brother as well. It was hard to pretend everything was normal, but my family was good at that.

At age thirteen, I remember my parents sitting me down at the dining room table. It was just me, dad, and my mother. I was the baby of the family. My older siblings were already out of the house. All except one, but he was not present. I remember looking at my mother and father, and it was clear something was drastically wrong. It was written all over their faces. What were they going to tell me? I was not prepared in any way for what was shared with me. My mother proceeded to tell me that she was leaving my father. That did not make any sense. How could this happen? We have a perfect family. They never fought. We spent time together on vacations. I loved them both dearly.

I knew by the look on my dad's face he did not want this. He was broken, tears streaming down his face. I felt this rage come over me. I expressed my opposition. No one was hearing me. I could not scream any louder. My only response was anger and to let them know I was not accepting this decision. I felt I could turn it around if I got angry enough and caused more disruption. I soon learned the decision was final. There was nothing I could do to get my family back. I felt abandoned. My life was torn apart. I did not want to live.

Things quickly got out of hand. I soon learned my mother left my father for my counselor. The guy who was supposed to help me ended up taking my mother away from my father. Talk about sick. I became belligerent towards authority of any kind. I was now going to do what I wanted to do when I wanted to do it. Everyone lost their right to tell me anything. I remember not having a solution for the anger and pain—what a powerless feeling. No one came to my rescue.

My older brother was already of age to drink. He would frequently have friends over and party. It sure looked fun. Drinking was always a part of my upbringing. My grandfather and uncles were always around the bar. I never saw the harm in it. My entire family was good at keeping things hidden. I often took a sip of beer when I was told to go fill it up. I am not sure when I first got drunk, but I know it happened. I eased my way into it. I do know that at some point, having started drinking, I began to explore marijuana. I just found my solution. School and sports were no longer a priority. Getting in trouble and getting high was already becoming a full-time job. I saw no danger in partying all the time.

This exploration progressed into other substances. I started exploring with other chemicals. If it was offered, I took it from alcohol to pot to LSD. Whatever felt good and took me out of myself was welcomed. At age sixteen, I started experimenting with heroin. I knew this was crossing a line. I remember what they taught us in school about these drugs. Heroin, however, felt entirely different. I truly found my match. There was no better feeling. From an angry, abandoned, troubled kid, I learned how to get rid of those feelings. This addiction progressed rather fast. Later that year, I was using more than my friends and found myself using intravenously. Things got out of hand real fast. I was on a mission. Every day was a job. When I started to get sick, I was driven to never feel that way

155

again. I would go to any length to make sure that never happened.

I turned to drug trafficking to supply my habit. This was a bad situation. I was sick. I was arrested in Philadelphia as a juvenile. I landed myself in jail for the first time. Needless to say, I was scared. I knew there was a problem, but the only solution was to get that substance into my body. I told them everything they wanted to hear. I just needed to get back out on the street. My poor father walked into the courtroom with tears in his eyes. In front of a judge, his youngest son strung out on heroin. I cannot imagine how he felt. He knew I was in trouble. He did the very best he could to hold the family together. I put him through literal hell. Addiction changes you. It turns you into someone you are not. It did not matter how or what stood in my way of the next one; I was getting it. The court ordered me to treatment and probation. As soon as I was released, I got high. I knew I only had a small window before probation would contact me.

I used as much as I could for the next few weeks. One morning I woke as usual. The first thing I did every day was to get high. There was nothing different here. I used that morning, and my next memory is waking up with tubes down my throat. The first words I said as I yanked the tubes out of my mouth were, "I do not have a problem." It shocked me that I said that, but it was the only thing I could say. It was an automatic response to the situation. I did not want anyone to know what was wrong with me. Deny everything. I was blind. I was a slave to my addiction. I had a serious problem and no solution.

I was taken to the hospital and then to my first treatment center. They took me in a wheelchair. I was maybe 120 pounds soaking wet. I was a sick kid. There was no denying the fact now. I desperately needed help, or I was going to die. Like any good addict, I hated treatment. For the first two weeks, I fought it. The problem was my probation officer saw it as necessary. I was forced to stay, and there was nothing I could do to change it.

This was the first time I learned about my addiction. I remember feeling a weight lifted off just knowing I was not the only one. Once I settled in, I responded well to their care. My family did whatever they could to love me through this very vulnerable time in my life. My parents would visit me. I was there for forty-two days. I needed longer. I did not get that sick overnight and did not heal that way either. I thought everything would be normal if I could just put the substance down. It did start the process.

I would like to say I stayed clean, and everything returned to normal. I still had to process my feelings again. I had not quite figured out the solution to those. I went to meetings and got a "name only sponsor." I never worked any steps. I relapsed after seven months. People, places, and things always got the best of me. I was back in treatment three months later. This time when I got out, I went after recovery.

I remember being in meetings for some time, and I started listening to this talk about a higher power. The concept was not new to me, nor did it cause me to become angry when people talked about God. I had very little understanding, and the version I had was warped from my childhood. However, as I listened, I knew that some people had some things right, and others seemed to come up with a higher power that let them live in old behaviors. This did not appeal to me. Something was happening inside, and God's grace began to seek me out. I worked a second shift job, and one night I recall seeing a calendar on the wall. It was a missionary calendar. I always had a heart for the least of these. My father instilled that in me. He always helped the forgotten. He was devout in his Catholic faith. I was grateful for that. I had real feelings for people.

I could see their pain. I left a sticky note on the calendar and returned to work the following day to find a sticky note in response. It said, "If you like this calendar, you should come to such and such a place at this time." I remember thinking this was odd, but something in me told me to go. A week later, I found myself driving to this unknown place for an unknown event. I had no idea what I was getting myself into. I remember there being a lot of men, like a few thousand. I did not look the part. I was a long-haired hippie kid. I sat in the top row, looking down over the auditorium.

I felt like an outsider, but something in me was stirring. I had this overwhelming feeling I needed to get as close to the stage as possible. There were no seats available. During an intermission, I stole a "biker for Jesus" seat. They were not happy with me. I was not moving, sorry. Out came the preacher. What I heard and felt in the next thirty minutes changed my life forever. The good news, the gospel I had never heard. Towards the end, I started to think that this entire evening was meant for me. Could this be true? I could not deny it. My heart was warmed to the presence of God. When the invitation was given, I felt a lump in my throat. It was not the tubes coming out this time. God loved me. He chose me. I was accepted just as I am. To say this was good news was an understatement. I knew there was nothing I could do to change or rectify my past. Why would God want anything to do with me? I had absolutely nothing to offer Him, but He had everything to offer me. Wow, at that very moment, I stood up and called out to God. Those "bikers for Jesus" men surrounded me as I surrendered my life to Jesus. Tears flowed from my eyes; I was weeping. I felt so sorry and yet so forgiven in the same moment.

My new life started after that moment. There was still so much confusion over what happened, but it was clear there was something different in me. My heart was changed. I had new desires within me. I had an energy to want to know more about God. His presence continued to draw me toward this new life. I wanted to learn about Jesus. Whatever happened that night, I wanted more of that. Not only that, but I wanted to tell everyone what happened. It was a spiritual experience. I heard about those in meetings but never understood what that meant. Sadly, I never heard of that experience in the meetings I was attending. When I returned to meetings, I wanted to share about my newfound faith. Most people did not take too well to this. I was actually pushed away. This was odd. I knew, though, what happened to me was real. I began to see these people were lost. They did not really know God. They had a version of God, but it was not the God I met. I could tell by their actions and speech. I was far from perfect, but I knew there was a difference.

God was now at work in me. He was starting to rearrange my desires, and my hunger for Him grew. I would spend the third shift after my job was complete reading a little New Testament Bible. I wanted to know more about Jesus. Strange feelings started. In one instance, I would desire God, and in the next, I would speak self-hatred at myself. I would hear voices in my mind telling me to kill myself. What was happening to me? I thought things were supposed to get better. Here is where I learned about my real enemy, and it wasn't my addiction. There was a dark side, and believe me, I knew it. I had practiced witchcraft as a young kid and involved myself in various occult practices. The devil was not letting go of his grip on me. I got involved in a local mission church, and this is where I met my wife. Her family recommended I see a Christian Counselor. I was willing to do whatever was necessary.

This counselor was a church fellow. What was he going to tell me? I always thought if you were to help me, you would have had to walk in my shoes. This was different. I was not seeking freedom from addiction but freedom from my tormented mind. I was having dreams of being possessed. I felt dark presences in my room. During these sessions, I began to understand what I learned was spiritual warfare. While seeing this counselor, I would tell him what was happening to me.

There was, in fact, a battle taking place. I was saved, no doubt, but there was still a battle for my mind, and if the devil could shut me down, he would render me powerless to live out this new faith. What I learned throughout my time with David was life transformational for me as a new believer. I learned "Who I was in Christ." I had been given a new identity when I placed my faith in Jesus.

From that moment, I was determined to tell others about this newfound gift. Learning God created me and God had given me purpose was profound. My counselor recommended a local church that was known for outreach. This was a rather large congregation, 1200 at the time. It did not take long for the pastor to reach out to me. Every week I brought recovering addicts into the church. That relationship with my pastor grew. We would meet weekly. During this time, I sensed a call in my life to full-time ministry. There was a college within our denomination that was well known and had a great program. I needed the training. It had been years since my brain worked like this.

Within two years, the church had raised money for me to attend Indiana Wesleyan University, and I was accepted on academic probation. My pastor believed in me, but I still doubted I could succeed. I still carried a self-defeating attitude with me. God used the next few years in my life. I loved learning about God and serving Him. It was powerful. During this time, I also married my wife, whom I had met a few years prior. She was eager to serve beside me in ministry. While away at school, I unintentionally disconnected from my pastor. To be honest, I had told God I would never end up back in Pennsylvania. I was determined to go elsewhere. Little did I know that self-will was taking back control. I soon became confused as to where God was leading me. I couldn't see myself being a pastor. I couldn't see myself doing anything in the local church. I was confused. During one of the summers at school, I had this idea to pick up a drink. Somehow, I had allowed a lie into my mind that alcohol was not my problem. I convinced my wife I would be fine. I had nine years sober at this point. What was a drink going to hurt? She had no idea, nor did she ever see me use. After I had spent days thinking about it, I convinced myself I was ok. I remember picking up and genuinely believing it would never go any further. Oh, the subtleness of addiction. Later that summer, before my junior year, I decided to leave the school. I was not cut out for ministry.

The next six years were whirlwind. I slowly fell away from God. At one point, there was a slight wake-up call when I tried to get back to church. I attended another online Bible college, but within two years, I was headed further away from God and His purposes for my life. We moved back to my home area of Sunbury, PA. I absolutely hated it, but we had no choice. We had our first child, and we were in debt. During this time, I worked for my family and then started a business serving food at music festivals all over the country. It was a last-ditch effort to survive. I can tell you God was just about non-existent in my life. I was living for myself and myself only, trying to get by. I kept my addiction under wraps for the most part. I was starting to use other substances at this point. If I could just vow to stay away from heroin, I would be ok. Every year that went by, I would fall farther away and allow things into my life that I would have never let in years prior. My heart was becoming hard again.

Once I started using hard drugs, it was all over. My poor wife had no idea what I was going to become. I started using drugs all the time. Not only on the road, but I was bringing them home. My wife slowly started to catch on. I was keeping her in denial as best I could. The last two years were utter hell. I was physically, mentally, and spiritually sick. Even those around me knew it. I tried to surround myself with people who had the same problem. As long as I did that, I had no accountability. I was angry at life and God. How could this happen? See, I was right. I was not worth it anyway. What would God want anything to do with a failure like me? I was eating pills all the time. It was a back-and-forth cycle daily, from speed to downers.

My wife slowly began to lose her mind. How could this happen? She started to confront my addiction. I did my best to avoid her, but she continued to put my addiction in my face. That February, I had a moment that broke me down. I honestly forgot how to feel. God's presence and grace were not evident. I knew God at one time, but now He was all but a memory and a very distant one. Sin and addiction will do that if you allow them to. I told my wife I needed help. I was so sick, and this would not end well if I continued down this path. My wife and son drove me to a treatment center that winter.

I hated it. I wanted to leave. I knew more than the counselors anyways. The truth was I forgot how to live without a drink or a drug. I did not even know who I was. During this time, God used an outside meeting to speak to me. It was a night meeting on the 3rd step. During the meeting, I remembered what God's voice had sounded like. It was what I needed to begin this journey again. I tried to listen to Christian worship music and had a slight moment one day with God where I confessed my need for Him again. I convinced my wife I could leave at the two-week mark. Actually, I told her I was leaving. I came back home and started going to meetings again. I had done this before, so I thought I had it figured out. I remained clean for the next five months. I still felt disconnected. I was not in church, nor was I truly seeking God. I was just trying to stay away from any mood-altering substances. My wife had a miscarriage that summer, and I used it as an excuse to pick up. There I was one evening, I wanted to use so I entertained the thought. I had a battle in my mind knowing it was wrong but allowed the idea to take root. I resisted one night and then fell the next. The next few months were a literal hell. I had driven myself to my lowest point. I was nearing death. I would use all night and all day. My relationship with my wife was broken beyond repair. I did not blame her. Although I knew deep down this was not what God had intended for us.

That fall, the only choice my wife had was to call an old friend who had been sober for two years. He was like a brother to me. She called him and said, "I'm not going to bury my husband." He left work immediately and drove up from Philadelphia to pick me up. I knew the tape was up. They were not going to let me continue down this path. I ended up detoxing in his basement. I was ready to give up. This relapsing was getting old. Why couldn't I stay sober? I stayed for two weeks and then returned home. Time will tell. What was I going to do?

There was a Big Daddy Weave concert at our church that coming week. I knew I had to be there. Towards the end of this concert, God's presence hit me like a ton of bricks. Everything came flooding back in. It was a moment I will never forget. I felt God again. He spoke to me just like he had so many years prior. I was dead, and when you hear God speak, you become alive in an instant. I re-surrendered my life to Jesus that night with my pastor behind me. I cried out to God with tears of repentance and sorrow for my life and the disappointment I had become. Did God still have a plan for my life? If not, I would still settle for anything but the life I had been living.

Over the next few years, I got reinvolved in AA and actually worked with a sponsor. I attended meetings daily and many times two times a day for a year. I worked the 12-steps and began to identify the causes and conditions of my spiritual sickness. I needed to stop playing God. I knew the correct answers. It was following through that was the problem. God had a plan, but I had decided what that plan would look like and what it wouldn't. When I told God years ago I would not return to the city and church I attended, that was me playing God and directing the show. My pastor met with me again and became my mentor. Did I lose my call to ministry? Was there still a plan for my life even though I had just thrown away the last fifteen years?

I soon realized God had not given up on me. I still felt strongly that I was to live my life in service to God. I had some work to do to prove myself faithful to His call on my life. After I had attended church and meetings for the next year or so, my pastor suggested I go back to school and finish the degree I had started many years ago. I only needed thirteen credits to graduate. It was part of my self-discipline. I needed to prove I would stick and stay. I was excited to be living again. I learned what had held me back from fully surrendering to God. I always said I gave 80% and held on to the other 20% just in case God did not work out. I always had a back door. I remember sensing God's voice saying it was not the 80% that kept me sick and away from him. It was the 20% I was holding back. Wow, that hit me. I was never fully surrendered to God. It was always contingent on my own desires and wants. That's not how service to God works.

At the two-year mark, I started having a vision for a church that would welcome drug addicts and alcoholics, but just how was my church going to reach these people? We were a large rural church, and rarely would you notice someone in our congregation that looked like they struggled with addiction. They were there, but it was not obvious. I come from a large congregation of around 2000 people. I started to see a vision for a church within the church, bridging the gap for those in recovery, providing them a safe place to seek and explore faith without all the extra stuff that is in a local church. Not that those things are bad, but that this kind of service would allow them to take in pieces at a time. I knew God wanted to meet people there. I remember my pastor thinking it was a great idea. I had no clue how it was going to come together. I lived in doubt for the following year.

I remember vividly one New Year's Day. We were discussing with my wife's family what it would look like to be fully surrendered to God. My wife and I had never allowed God to use us in whatever capacity He chose. Service was always what we wanted it to be. It was at that time my wife and I decided to give Jesus full control over our life and ministry. We told God we would go wherever he sent us. We did not want to waste this life. We already threw away so many years running on self-will. During this time, I had also been at a faith-based coalition meeting, and Pastor Max Ingram was giving a presentation on Recovery Church. I was intrigued. I remember looking up the Recovery Church Movement and reading word for word the vision God had laid on my heart to serve as a bridge between the local church and those in recovery. It was word for word what I had envisioned. I was not ready for such a commitment but knowing someone else was doing this kind of church was great.

Later that year, my heart and my wife's heart were burning to serve the Lord. I had finished all the hard work of school. I had a great relationship with my pastor and my sponsor. We were ready to find a place to serve. My wife and I visited a church that winter when God reminded us of the type of ministry He was calling us to. We wanted to see broken people walking into the church. We wanted to see the hand of God changing those who were labeled as the lepers of society. We felt called to that church for a time and went as far as to meet with the pastoral team about a potential job. I had no idea how God would work out the details, and we didn't care. We just wanted to give everything to God and serve the broken.

The following few months were filled with an excitement that we never had. We saw a new vision and a plan. Everything in us believed this was where God was leading us. Then Covid happen. It completely shut down the world and left God's apparent call on our lives in limbo. Now what? I had a plan, sensed God's leading, and then nothing. Why does God not make sense sometimes?

During that summer, we took some much-needed time off. Life paused for a moment. To be honest, I checked out. I had no clue how God would work, and it seemed like I had a few months to relax and not try to figure it out. When we returned home from summer vacation, my wife and I were overcome by discouragement. I trusted God; that was never a doubt. I just could not see His hand at work at this moment. The big question was, now what? During the next forty days, I felt God calling me to fast. I had never fasted before, at least not to this level. I was reading a book by Andrew Murray and felt the Lord speaking to me about "Waiting on Him," not waiting on something from God but simply "Waiting on God." Regardless of where we would be or end up, what was important was for me to stay connected to God and simply feast on His goodness in my life and my family. God was preparing something, but that was not to be my focus for the next forty days. I had to give up my plans and what I hoped them to be. The Lord asked me to set aside any desires of my own and only desire Him. I am naturally undisciplined, but I stuck to my fast and spent the next forty days letting my "Yes be yes and my no be no." I only wanted God. My prayer was that He does in me what I can never accomplish by my own strength. Restore to me the joy of my salvation.

Coming out of this time of prayer and fasting, we started visiting the local church where I had met my wife. We sensed God moving there. They had people who struggled with addictions. At least I knew who God wanted me to reach. Our current church was going through a transition. The senior pastor who was my mentor for years was retiring. A new pastor was taking his place. There were a lot of decisions up in the air. I was seriously thinking about joining this other church and their mission, although we were not entirely convinced that's where God wanted us.

Within two weeks, I was contacted by Pastor Branden Mestach of Christ Wesleyan Church. I knew little about Pastor Brandon. I will never forget that meeting. I heard Pastor Brandon's heart for the broken, especially those who struggled with drug and alcohol addiction. Pastor Brandon and his wife Nikki had lost Nikki's brother Ike seven years prior to a heroin overdose. Pastor Brandon wanted this type of ministry at Christ Wesleyan Church. He and the senior pastor had discussed what this would look like, and they both believed in me and God's call on my life. We had some major decisions to make. He was going to be the new senior pastor and began to speak to me about my vision for recovery ministry.

Over the next two weeks, God made it clear where we were to be. My heart was always there; I just struggled to see how a rural church could do ministry to people who lived outside of our immediate reach. Well, the church had a campus in Sunbury, PA, with little vision. They inherited it and tried to do a satellite campus. It was accomplishing that purpose, but the future was unknown. After I was hired on as a "Recovery Pastor," I began speaking to Pastor Brandon about "Recovery Church." That was still my heart. I saw it happening in Sunbury. That is the town I long before told God I would never return. Funny how God works. We wanted to be where there was the greatest need. Ministry has nothing to do with what we think we should do or where we should be. If this vision was going to happen, it would only be by the hand of God. I met with Pastor Brandon and began to pitch the vision. He was on board. He loved the idea. The next step was meeting with Pastor Phil Dvorak from Recovery Church Movement. I never wanted to be on my own island. I believed in Phil's vision for Recovery Church. We wanted to be part of something that has the potential to change the world. They have the people and resources to really impact the Kingdom.

After a few meetings, we knew this was where God wanted us. We set a launch date for later that summer and began to prepare. So much preparation had already been done, especially within our hearts. We launched with twenty-five people in August of 2021. This August marks one year. We have seen God do an amazing work in Sunbury, PA. We average eighty in attendance and had over one-hundred people for our baptism service. We have heard so many testimonies of people coming to Jesus. We are seeing families restored and relationships healed. God is at work. He is just getting started. We have over fifty people serving in worship and other volunteer positions. God is giving us a purpose of reaching those who are lost in addiction with the good news that Jesus is able to completely save those whom He calls out of addiction and sin. He truly sets us free. Our community is a growing family. We love the Recovery Church Movement. God is bringing revival to our community and local church. Recovering addicts set free through Jesus Christ have a powerful

story to proclaim. Let it be spoken on every street and every city in America that Jesus Saves!!!

Deb's Story
The Family Disease

Choice is a gift God gives us. The question begs: do you accept this challenge of choosing? Do you choose God's path or your path? His grace has accompanied me and provided healing and restoration along the way. I have participated in recovery most of my life. I'm sixty-seven and have enjoyed personal sobriety for over forty-eight years. Recovery has been a gift from God, who has continually provided me with a fresh perspective at every intersection along my journey.

Just as I feel certain the sun will rise every morning, I, too, feel certain the sun will set; I know that I know Jesus Christ's steadfast love will sustain me all the days of my journey. "The steadfast love of the Lord never ceases; His mercies never come to an end: they are new every morning; great is your faithfulness. 'The LORD is my portion,' says my soul, 'therefore, I will hope in Him.'" (Lamentations 3:22-24 ESV).

God has given me with an endless supply of determination, courage, and enthusiasm for the long recovery process. I have experienced many choices of starting over. I'm convinced this journey of recovery isn't for the faint of heart. Self-honesty and the willingness to change have been my constant companions keeping my heart continuously pliable by God. Faith in God has sustained me through the tragedies of my life. My life began trapped inside a horrifically dysfunctional family with a charming alcoholic father at the helm; lies, sin, confusion, and desperation drove me into the arms of my Savior.

My entire life was confusing because there was the cold, stark truth and yet an aura everyone operated from, full of denial, isolation, fear, and lack of identity. Two worlds were co-existing where blame and truth couldn't be discussed or recognized. I fought against acquiring my father's mindset from a very early age, and I was determined not to become him. I knew he appeared charming, and yet his behavior was that of an insane person. My father's actions were overlooked. He participated in extramarital affairs, leaving the family for months on end while he was on a bender. I experienced verbal, physical, and sexual abuse from a man who, all the while, was sharing the gospel through singing and praising Jesus. My mind was filled with confusing thoughts, realizations, and ruminations which provoked mistrust, but prepared me to take charge and search for tools to navigate life.

I was often referred to as "his little boy he never had," which meant trips to the barber shop for haircuts, shirtless until I was nine or ten. He took me on car rides where he manipulated my mind to feel sorry for him and to understand he needed my secrecy. Because my parents had an unhappy marriage, they didn't sleep together; rather, I slept with my father. I prayed he would leave again for another bender or just leave. Soon he left for the final time, leaving me in charge of my mom's final years with her struggle with advanced colon cancer. I was near the end of my first year of high school when I dropped out in desperation to be with her and in great denial of her impending death. I was confused due to the amount of pot I was smoking, the use of speed to stay up at night with her in the hospital, and downers to take the edge off and occasionally close my eyes. I felt trapped with adult responsibilities while only possessing the mind of a child. My body craved the self-medication physically, mentally, and emotionally.

As I sunk further into addiction, I made it through her funeral and the deep beginning stages of grief until God awakened me from a deep sleep (both metaphorically and in reality) and asked me to follow Him. At two AM, I proceeded to follow what I knew was His directive. I poured the drugs down the toilet, the alcohol down the sink, cleaned my apartment, and began a walk with Jesus at the age of nineteen. I have never forgotten his words, "follow me, and I will use you." I had no idea, but my soul was awakened. I took the GED and began working three jobs to pay past debt and to get myself into college.

It's a Family Disease. I have done a healthy 4th step multiple times, and been forced to look at the dysfunction of my family of origin. I recognized my harmful behavior as an overprotective parent with great honesty and have admitted my own sin and imperfections of distrust. Right when I thought things were beginning to go smoothly, or I had been through what seemed to be the most difficult parts of my journey (addiction, loss of my mother, career changes, working multiple jobs ultimately becoming a successful entrepreneur, working long hours to climb the corporate ladder, marrying the wrong person and enduring divorce), life took another unexpected turn when I became ill with an autoimmune disease in which I would fluctuate between remission and exacerbation. It was as confusing as the road of addiction and recovery, and I'm convinced the two diseases parallel each other.

We are only as sick as our secrets. As life was beginning to go well and a successful business established, I then married Mr. Wonderful, aka Don. I established restrictions and rules pertaining to drugs, alcohol, and "the one mistake plan only," meaning one affair and it's over. I was a chick in charge; however, I failed to be totally honest about my past because I didn't know how to do that. I was in denial and had firm boundaries about everything, and control was my go-to language.

Life is good, my husband is nothing like my father, the Christmas photos are beautiful, the marriage is blessed and ordained by God, life is full, and family is happening. We have six beautiful children, all with their own life calling from Jesus. There was only one parenting book I used, and boy did I thump it - at them. I was convinced I would raise Christians devoted to Christ with no family dysfunction (exercising much control of outcomes). Their lives would be different than mine. They would thank me one day, or so I thought. It appears I put the D in dysfunction. Through my self-imposed religious devotion, I was rule-bound and self-driven. I tried with all my might, keyword "my" to live a good life. I imparted this with much enthusiasm, not recognizing an adult child of an alcoholic has come to the table with her own issues.

Thank God for the twelve steps, ACA (Adult Child of an Alcoholic), and a wonderful psychologist who helped me at age fifty-seven to admit for the first time that which I just shared with you. We were able to make sense of the confusion, begin to see why I had become a hypervigilant protector, demander of truth, control freak, and recognize and begin to heal the scared young child within. I was exhausted in that I had an overdeveloped sense of responsibility for anyone and everyone. I came to realize the demands on my children and the reality of what I was trying to control in my efforts to make them "a perfect Christian like me."

It was not until my kids began to fight their own addictions and travel their own journeys that I recognized my fear of their becoming addicts and alcoholics. I had carried this fear my entire life. Life began to be unmanageable, from a place in my heart I couldn't face. With God's help, I had been able to stop my drinking, but I questioned if they could manage their own demons, and worse was the thought if I had passed on this generational curse. The "what if's" were almost too big for me. I loved them with great passion. As a child of an alcoholic, I couldn't face the fear of abandonment of our family values and love, that they would live their lives crippled by addiction and perhaps not survive. My stint with drugs and alcohol was short-lived compared to those who battle this disease for many long years, but I became a "dry drunk" or a para-alcoholic, meaning the characteristics of the disease had not been healed.

I believe God placed me in the rooms of AA many times

for myself, not just for the ones I was there supporting. My deliverance from a lifelong illness was arrested while suffering the concerns of my family members. It has taken a lifetime for me to heal, and He is still healing me day by day. It truly is a LIFETIME journey of recovery.

At fifty, I retired from my career to work for God. I have attended seminary, received my master's in biblical counseling, and will soon complete my doctorate. Working as a pastor, counselor, and lover of souls has brought me to a place of healing and forgiveness. I love watching God work in the lives of others. I have learned to trust God with my family, and I know His plans are His, and I only get to participate prayerfully, not play God. A few years ago, I met Pastor Phil, we immediately became the closest of friends, and I fell in love with Recovery Church. I felt "I had come home." I met many of you and realized you are family! You are my brothers and sisters in Christ, and we are all walking the journey of healing and recovery together. There is no place I'd rather be than in communion with all of you.

Bruce's Story
The Wretch

"Amazing GRACE HOW SWEET THE SOUND...THAT SAVED A WRETCH LIKE ME...I ONCE WAS LOST, BUT NOW, I'M FOUND...WAS BLIND, BUT NOW I SEE."

My name is Bruce, and the above song lyrics are the soundtrack to my life. From the moment of conception, I have been in survival mode. Born to a fifteen-year-old alcoholic mother, my grandmother got custody of me at eight months old. When I went to live with her, I was the seventeenth child of ten boys and seven girls. Of the seventeen already, fourteen of the children were alcoholics. I grew up in an absurd, dysfunctional, violent household, one you could not even imagine. Alcohol strongly impacted my life before I even took my first drink, as did drugs. Violence was prevalent. Alcohol, drugs, and violence became the story of my life.

Uncles also lived in this home, and they were the most physically and emotionally abusive men you could imagine. My biological mother was just as bad, maybe even more so. The stories of my past range from molestations to murder. I was regularly violated by the very people responsible for my care and well-being. Nights for me were long and lonely, and often I would just wish for the daytime to never end. Why? Because the darkness was not my friend.

At the age of eleven years old I witnessed a man rape my mom. Seeing this, I felt both helpless and enraged. This man would go to jail and get released two weeks later. One day, not long after, as I was getting out of school, I saw this man standing on the street corner drinking and laughing along with some other men. It was at that moment I decided to go home, get a gun, and followed the man to a secluded area. It was there that I shot him in the head.

I was charged as a juvenile as I was just turning twelve and spent two years in a juvenile facility. The damage had been done. My life would never be savable. My downward trajectory would be just beginning, but it would gain speed. I would go to prison, where I would commit violent acts, and upon my release, that would be all I knew, and I was now only seventeen years of age.

One day while running with the wrong crowd (the right crowd for me), I found myself in a situation where there was gunfire erupting between two groups, and a three-year-old child was innocently killed. I was charged with felony murder and offered a life sentence for the offense. I knew I had not pulled the trigger but was just as guilty or responsible by being with the wrong crowd.

It was at this time that I cried out for God, and He heard me. I would go to trial for the charges and found myself acquitted of all charges. But what now? I would begin an arduous and painful life. Waiting for the trial, I spent two years in prison. Upon release, I would begin to use drugs and alcohol to medicate myself from my life of pain and loneliness. At the age of twenty, I was a full-blown heroin addict and would not stop until I was forty-eight years of age. For twenty-eight years, life was a living hell. I was depressed, suicidal, and homicidal. You could just see it on me and through my behavior.

I would go on to do five prison bids. I destroyed all relationships living a dangerous, selfish, self-centered existence. I cannot even now share my nickname from those days. I was coming to the end. I was desperate, defeated, and ready to die. But God had a different plan!

That life came to an end on December 20th, 2021. I had come to my wit's end. The evening before, I had sat in my car, crying, with a gun to my head ready to take my life, when I heard a voice. The Lord was speaking to me, saying, "GO." It was a gentle whisper, "GO." At that moment, I remembered a book I had read while incarcerated as a juvenile. The book was titled "Came to Set the Captives Free." At that moment, I knew that it was HIS way of saying, "You have created and built this self-imposed prison around yourself over these many years, BUT I came to set the captives (you) free."

At that moment, I got on the expressway and drove to Florida. The trip was painstaking. It was twelve hours from home, and I wanted to turn around a hundred times. Yet all I could think about was the pain that was behind me, and I began to be filled with a spirit of freedom in front of me. That visualization kept me going.

I knew of a way to freedom in Vero Beach, and I kept moving forward. I soon would be introduced to Recovery Church Vero Beach. It was awesome and one of the best introductions and experiences of my life! Through RCVB, for the very first time in my life, I experienced love, connection, and belonging. I knew at that moment I was experiencing what God had for me, what some people never get to experience. But why me? I learned God had a plan for me. I experienced a new family who loved me, and it continued all around me.

I gave my life to the Lord and was baptized in the Holy Spirit, and now I have a family at Recovery Church, for which I will be forever grateful. I would not trade them for the world.

I write this grateful and thankful to God for speaking to me at that moment I wanted to end my life. I am thankful for my new family, my new life, and the opportunity to share this story with you. Today I know this...GOD has always been speaking to me. I just didn't listen. It wasn't that He was not loud enough. It was because I was never quiet or humble enough.

His Vision
The Already but not Yet

A Recovery Church in every city in this nation and beyond.

And they have defeated him by the blood of the Lamb and by the word of their testimony. And they did not love their lives so much that they were afraid to die. (Revelations 12:11 NLT)

Addiction is the devil's home turf. He loves what addiction does. The great accuser has been running amuck since before the Garden. However, the word of God tells us that he is a defeated adversary. He is defeated by the blood of the Lamb and the word of "our" testimony. And "we" did not love "our" lives so much that "we" were afraid to die. Three quick ideas here: blood of the lamb, word of their testimony, and they were not afraid to die.

Blood of the Lamb. It's all about Jesus. Jesus isn't an option; He's the way, the truth, and the life. Without Jesus, there is no hope. Our hope is found in Jesus and Jesus alone. When I was first coming to faith, I heard the song "There is power, power, wonder working power in the precious blood of the Lamb" (Jones, 1899). Those words sounded so strange to me, honestly a bit repulsive. I didn't understand the comparison of Jesus to the Passover lamb. All of it seemed like foolishness. However, now those words are like sweet music to my ears. Everything changes when we understand it's not about us, but His finished work on the cross. It's about how a holy God can take something as vile as the brutal murder of His son and make it the most beautiful thing in all of history. When we serve a God like that, we can have faith that he can restore and redeem us.

Word of their testimony. There is power in your story. People can argue with your theology, your beliefs, your thoughts, and ideas, but it's tough to argue with our testimony. All of creation hangs on the Word of God. When we share how our story became a part of God's story, eternity is transformed. Recovery

Church is a collection of these stories. Stories of how God reaches into the middle of our darkest moments and rescues us.

Not afraid to die. There is something so powerful when someone has faced death and been brought back to the fullness of life. Redeemed addicts and alcoholics fully devoted to the mission of the Kingdom are an unstoppable army. When we are totally surrendered to God, the fear of death no longer controls us. I'm not talking about some prideful courage. But a peace which allows a person to stay focused on the mission of the Gospel. It's such a rare, beautiful thing when you find someone so at peace with God, they have no fear of death. Of course, most people are a little nervous about the mystery of eternity and maybe even the process of dying. However, in the midst of that nervousness, there are some people whose faith is so rooted in Christ that "death has lost its sting." They understand in a profound way the word of Paul when he says to "live is Christ to die is gain" (Philippians 1:21).

A good friend and legal counsel for Recovery Church introduces himself when he attends recovery meetings, "Hi, my name is T, and I love my life." When you first hear him say this, you might be a bit bewildered; I know I was. After a few moments, like a joke that you were the last one to get, "oh, I get it." You see, the ultimate idol many of us have is ourselves, our own life. As Bonhoeffer stated, the Christian path and for us the way to recover, 'When Christ calls a man, he bids him come and die.' As Bill Wilson, one of the founders of Alcoholics Anonymous, called it "ego deflation at depth." And of course, the best one of all, Jesus said, "pick up your cross and follow me."

What is required of a person to start this journey we call recovery? "The first requirement is that we be convinced that any life run on self-will can hardly be a success" (Alcoholics Anonymous World Services, p. 60). When a new addict or alcoholic begins this recovery journey, many come with a straightforward goal to stop using. They just want the insanity to stop. They are confused and desperate, but most never dream that staying sober would mean that they only need to "change one thing and that one thing is everything." The whole program of recovery is about removing us from the center of the story. When you reflect on your life, you are often the center of that narrative; we all are. Our narcissism is deeply ingrained. If a movie of your life were made, we all would cast ourselves as the lead role. But the problem is we can't all be the star. "Each person is like an actor who wants to run the whole show; is forever trying to arrange the lights, the ballet, the scenery, and the rest of the players in his own way. If his arrangements would only stay put, if only people would do as he wished, the show would be great. Everybody, including himself, would be pleased. Life would be wonderful." (Alcoholics Anonymous World Services, p. 60).

"This is the how and why of it. First of all, we had to quit playing God. It didn't work. Next, we decided that hereafter in this drama of life, God was going to be our Director. He is the Principal; we are His agents. He is the father, and we are His children. Most good ideas are simple, and this concept was the keystone of the new and triumphant arch through which we passed to freedom" (Alcoholics Anonymous World Services, p. 62). We are all part of a much better, much larger, much more majestic story. Yes, you are valuable, more valuable than you can fully fathom, but it's not about you. It's about God. "Selfishness - self-centeredness! That, we think, is the root of our troubles. Driven by a hundred forms of fear, self-delusion, self-seeking, and self-pity..." (Alcoholics Anonymous World Services, p. 62). That is the heart of the journey for those caught in addiction. A movement from self-will, from looking within an individual, to a solution that is found in total surrender of our will back to the beginning, God. "So our troubles, we think, are basically of our own making. They arise out of ourselves, and the alcoholic is an extreme example of self-will run riot, though he usually doesn't think so. Above everything, we alcoholics must be rid of this selfishness. We must, or it kills us! God makes that possible" (Alcoholics Anonymous World Services, p. 62).

There is a prayer that millions of alcoholics and addicts are encouraged to pray during their recovery journey. This prayer is often referred to as the Third Step Prayer. I can only imagine how His Church and this world would be transformed if every believer lived out this prayer.

> *The Third Step Prayer* - "God, I offer myself to Thee-to build with me and to do with me as Thou wilt. Relieve me of the bondage of self, that I may better do Thy will. Take away my difficulties, that victory over them may bear witness to those I would help of Thy Power, Thy Love, and Thy Way of life. May I do Thy will always!" (Alcoholics Anonymous World Services, p. 63)

At Recovery Church, we refer to this process as 12-Steps One-Goal. The goal of recovery is not just to stop using drugs and alcohol. While this may be a benefit, it is not the goal. Step Twelve: "Having had a spiritual awakening as the result of these steps, we tried to carry this message to alcoholics and to practice these principles in all our affairs."

The result of the steps is a spiritual awakening which is lived out and shared with others. This sounds a lot like being "born again" and the "Great Commission."

> "When we sincerely took such a position, all sorts of remarkable things followed. We had a new Employer. Being all powerful, He provided what we needed, if we kept close to Him and performed His work well. Established on such a footing we became less and less interested in ourselves, our little plans, and designs. More and more we became interested in seeing what we could contribute to life. As we felt new power flow

in, as we enjoyed peace of mind, as we discovered we could face life successfully, as we became conscious of His presence, we began to lose our fear of today, tomorrow or the hereafter. We were reborn." (Alcoholics Anonymous World Services, p. 63).

A side effect or a residual benefit of following "The Way" are some fantastic things: families restored, lives changed, more love, more joy, more peace, more patience, more self-control, God's favor might even fall on you. But we need to be careful not to reduce this journey to playing a country music song backward. "You get your wife back, your kids back, your job back, car back, etc." The goal of Recovery Church, and I might argue most twelve-step fellowships, is for God's people to return to their Heavenly Father through Jesus. Our journey isn't about us. It's about Him. "Without help, it is too much for us. But there is One who has all power—that One is God. May you find Him now!" (Alcoholics Anonymous World Services, p. 59).

Redeemed alcoholics and addicts in recovery are some of the best people you could ever do ministry with. They have stared evil in the eyes, witnessed destruction, committed horrific acts, and lost at times more than we could understand. However, they've been rescued and given a new life. This literal death to life experience gives them a boldness in faith which is often missing among many others in the Church.

Recovery Church was birthed reluctantly with really very little vision or faith. We now believe RC was pushed forward by a holy God who is willing to do unbelievable things to see his children restored to him. The word kairos is Greek for "opportunity" or "fitting time." The term kairos is used in a few places in Scripture. It says in Mark 1:15, "The time is fulfilled, and the kingdom of God is at hand; repent and believe in the gospel." Our world is in crisis. Believers could look at this time and try to protect and save what they have. Or we could look at this time as a kairos moment—a moment where the opportunity to advance the Kingdom has never been more apparent. We believe Recovery Church is sitting at a Kairos moment. The harvest has never been more plentiful. As the world becomes more desperate, the opportunity increases, and the mission becomes more critical.

Somewhere around 2019, we started saying yes to new Recovery Churches. We went from that one tiny outpost to two to three, to six, to ten, to eighteen, to over thirty in more than a dozen states. We are well over 1000 addicts and alcoholics gathering each week with hundreds coming to faith and being baptized.

Our faith and our vision have increased. We've grown from an idea, to a network of Recovery Churches, to the groanings of a movement. We now hold to a God-sized vision because we have seen Him do what only He could do. We are witnessing God raising up disciple-makers within the recovery community and starting, planting, and reproducing Recovery Churches. People who were lost in their addictions, who everyone thought the last chapter had been written, have seen God change the narrative. A story of destruction has become His story of redemption. These stories have increased our faith and vision.

We now have the vision to see a Recovery Church in every city in this nation and beyond. Not because we need the name of Recovery Church to spread, but because people are dying without knowing Jesus and a path to Recovery. We believe that we will see countless families restored and generational curses broken. We believe nothing will bring God more honor than for all the world to hear how a Holy God went through extravagant measures to reach the junkie, drunk, crack head, outcasts, sinners, wayward children, the lepers of today- us. We believe that we will witness redeemed addicts and alcoholics lead a revival in this nation and beyond. That the lepers of today are healed in such miraculous ways that it's undeniably God at work. This world is changed because a group of alcoholics, knowing the blood of the Lamb covers them, begin to share the word of their testimony with boldness and without fear. We believe because of this faith, we will see people recover from a seemingly hopeless state of mind, be brought to purpose for God and see eternity changed for His glory. This is His Story of Recovery Church.

EPILOGUE

God is still writing the Story of Recovery Church. We are a beautiful, messy family. From the time of our initial drafts of this text, our fellowship has continued to increase in size, complexity, and impact. Many more people who were lost in their addictions have come to faith in Jesus and found a path of recovery.

Our story is real, raw, and unrefined. We have intentionally included stories in this text that might not be the most refined literary works or express a textbook path of recovery or even perfect theology. Sometimes when people share their testimonies of faith and recovery, it can be misinterpreted that everything post surrendering to Jesus and starting recovery is all "sunshine and rainbows." This is simply not true. Yes, there are blessings and amazing stories of restoration. However, addiction and sin can leave scars that might never fully be healed on this side of eternity. We have included people's stories who have, since the initial writing, gone on to plant more Recovery Churches and who have had marriages and families restored. However, we have also included stories of our family members who have since relapsed. We believe that our strength is in our rigorous honesty, even in our weaknesses.

We believe that, as the next chapters of His Story of Recovery Church are written, God is going to do immeasurably more than all we ask or imagine, according to His power that is at work within us. To Him be the glory in the church and in Christ Jesus throughout all generations, forever and ever. Amen

APPENDIXES

Who We Are & What We Do:

Recovery Church Movement (RCM) is a network of Recovery Churches reaching and training those in early recovery to grow in their faith and recovery. RCM is a bridge between the 12-Step Fellowships and the Church. We train, coach, and help people learn to become disciple makers within the recovery community and start, plant, and reproduce Recovery Churches.

Vision:

A Recovery Church in every city in this nation and beyond.

Mission:

Equipping God's people to do God's work of Recovery.

Non-Negotiables

Values:

UNITY

There is diversity in our unity – All are welcome to be a part of the Recovery Church family. No matter what a person believes or doesn't believe, what they have done or not done, the color of their skin, their education, or lack thereof, all are a part of the Recovery Church family. We are made different because you are a part of us. We may be diverse, but we are united in our shared solution. We are united with the Church - We are for the Church. We desire to be a resource to the local and global Church. We encourage our Recovery Church family to be a part of the local and global Church. We don't care who gets the credit, so long as God gets the glory. We are for all 12-step fellowships. We are for recovery. We encourage our family members to be active members in other 12-steps fellowships (i.e., AA/NA/CA/CR/SA, etc.)

RECOVERY

We do recover. One of our key purposes is to recover and help other alcoholics and addicts to recover. As we recover, we grow to be more like Jesus. One moment at a time. One step at a time. One day at a time. God's ultimate purpose for our life is that We will be conformed to the image of Jesus Christ. We can experience freedom from eternal death because Jesus lives in us but also the freedom to live an abundant life free from the bondage of addiction in the present because Jesus lives through us. With the indwelling of the Holy Spirit, we are equipped to fight the temptations of the future.

JESUS

Jesus isn't an option; He's the way, the truth, and the life. Without Jesus, there is no hope. Our hope is found in Jesus and Jesus alone. "God is everything or else He is nothing. God either is, or He isn't," and Jesus is God with us. We believe that Jesus is the Christ, God incarnate. He came in human form to sacrifice Himself, once and for all, that we might not perish but have eternal life. This is the bedrock of our belief.

BIBLE

The Bible (The Old and New Testaments) is the divine standard for what we believe, teach, and do. Inspired by God and a complete revelation of His Will for the salvation of men. Knowing and obeying God's Word is fundamental to all true success.

SERVICE

We joyfully serve the Lord and our neighbors. We desire to be spiritual contributors, not consumers. "Faith without works is dead." We are called to carry the message of faith and recovery and will do "anything short of sin" to "help reach a fellow sufferer." Service of this kind will mean sacrifice (John 15:13). We give of our time, treasure, and talent and live boldly with a principle of generosity in all our affairs. We long to hear the words. "Well done, good and faithful servant!"

COMMUNITY

We value and are a part of the greater Community and therefore work with people, organizations, and churches to help serve others in and out of recovery. We are a community of men and women who "share their experience, strength and hope with each other" that God "may solve our common problem and help others to recover." We "are responsible when any addict or alcoholic reaches out for help." We want the hands and feet of Jesus to always be there, and for that, we are responsible.

STEPS

We work the 12-Steps. The 12-Steps embody many of the Bible's core teachings related to God's redemptive work and man's response. A thorough working of the steps will lead a person to a more abundant life (free from the enslavement of addiction), closer to God and others.

ROTATION

A spirit of Rotation helps to ensure that "we serve and don't rule." Our leaders are but trusted servants. With no "status" at stake, we have complete freedom to serve as we are needed. We strive for collective responsibility, not personal authority. God opposes the proud but shows favor to the humble. Humility is at the center of our efforts. Jobs may have titles. But titles in Recovery Church do not bring Power or Control; they reflect our giftings, callings, services, and responsibilities. We encourage all active servants to serve in twos and threes. We ask the question, "who is in front of you, and who is behind you?" We actively train our replacements and release new leaders.

PRAYER

We will be known as a people of prayer. Prayer keeps us humble. Reminds us that it is not us but God who restores us to sanity. Prayer is the primary work of God's people. We believe that nothing of lasting value can be done unless it is bathed in prayer.

RAW

We are a peculiar people, led and empowered by the Spirit. Recovery Church is raw, unrefined, and with no pretense. God's purposes mean taking faith-filled risks. This almost always involves change.

DISCIPLESHIP / SPONSORSHIP

We cannot do this alone. We recover together. We see sponsorship as a great opportunity for discipleship. We encourage all Recovery Church family members to have a sponsor, when ready, to sponsor others, and teach those they are sponsoring to do the same. As Christians, we are commanded to go make disciples and teach them to obey the commands of Christ. Completing the Great Commission will require the mobilization of every fully devoted disciple.

LOVE

God is Love. We will be known for our love. Without love, we are nothing, just a noisy gong. We will love others boldly because Christ first loved us.

What We Believe:

IN ESSENTIAL BELIEFS: WE HAVE UNITY

"There is one Body and one Spirit...one Lord, one faith, one baptism, and one God and Father of us all" Ephesians 4:4-6

THE ESSENTIALS WE BELIEVE:

The following is a summary list of what Recovery Church considers to be the essential beliefs. This is not intended to be an exhaustive theology, however, a brief overview of the essential doctrine of the Christian faith. Removing any one of these items could lead to false doctrine and teaching. They are all essential, foundational, and necessary.

THE TRINITY (GODHEAD)

There is one God, co-existent, co-equal, and co-eternal in three persons: Father, Son, and Holy Spirit. (Deut. 6:4). Christianity teaches that God is Triune (Trinity), which means, God is one and in three persons: God the Father, God the Son, and God the Holy Spirit. This view of God is different than any other view of God in the world. No other religion teaches that their god is one and exists in three persons.

THE FATHER

The first person of the Trinity orders and directs all things according to His purpose and pleasure. He authored, created, and sustains all things in the universe without any means other than His pure nature and power. By His grace, He involves Himself in the affairs of men, hears and answers prayer, and saves from sin and death all that come to Him through Jesus Christ. Mt. 6:9, Eph. 1:3, John. 5:19.

THE LORD JESUS CHRIST

He exists eternally as the second person of the Trinity. By His virgin birth, He came to Earth as fully God and fully man, living a sinless life. He authored, created, and sustains all things in the universe. His death on the cross, paid the penalty for man's sin, evidenced by His bodily resurrection from the dead. He physically ascended to the right hand of God the Father, and He will return in power and glory. John. 1:14, Col. 2:9, Act. 2:33, Col. 1:16.

THE HOLY SPIRIT

He exists eternally as the third person of the Trinity. He convicts men of sin, regenerates, baptizes, indwells, instructs, and sets apart believers unto a holy life. We encourage all believers to seek a life of obedience to the leadership of the Holy Spirit. The Holy Spirit is God. Tit. 3:5, Act. 1:8, 1 Cor. 3:16.

THE BIBLE

The Scriptures of the Old and New Testaments are the complete, divinely inspired, trustworthy Word of God. The Bible is the authority and guide for our Christian faith and living. (2 Pet. 1:20, Heb. 4:12).

THE NATURE OF MANKIND

Mankind was directly created in God's image. He voluntarily fell into sin by personal disobedience to the will of God; as a result, all people are spiritually dead apart from Jesus Christ. The effect of the fall spread to all men, each of whom is born with a sinful nature and is in need of salvation. (Eph. 2:1, Rom. 3:10, Rom. 3:23-24).

THE NECESSITY OF SALVATION

Salvation is by grace, a gift of God apart from works. Salvation includes repentance, a turning from one's own way to God's way. All who receive Jesus Christ are born-again, made new by the Holy Spirit, and become the children of God. Our relationship with Christ is secure not by our actions but by the sustaining power and love of God. A changed life follows the work of God in a person's salvation. (Tit. 2:11, 1 John. 1:9, 1 Pet. 2:2).

THE CHURCH

The church is the body of believers consisting of all born-again persons without respect to race, culture, age, or background. Directed by Jesus Christ and empowered by the Holy Spirit, the church is taking the Good News to the whole world. Our fellowship stresses love for God and one another, the unity of all believers, and obedience to the Holy Spirit. (Eph. 2:19-21, Eph. 3:10).

ABOUT ETERNITY

People were created to exist forever. We will either exist eternally separated from God by sin or eternally with God through forgiveness and salvation. To be eternally separated from God is Hell. To be eternally in union with Him is eternal life. (John. 3:16; 14:17; Rom. 6:23; 8:17-18; Rev.20:15; 1 Cor. 2:7-9).

IN NON-ESSENTIAL BELIEFS: WE HAVE LIBERTY

"Accept him whose faith is weak, without passing judgment on disputable matters... Who are you to judge someone else's servant? To his own master he stands or falls... So whatever you believe about these things keep between yourself and God." (Romans 14:1, 4, 12, 22).

IN ALL OUR BELIEFS: WE SHOW CHARITY

"If I have the gift of prophecy and can fathom all mysteries and all knowledge, and if I have a faith that can move mountains, but have not love, I am nothing." (1 Corinthians 13:2).

Processes:

The Recovery Church Movement is a learning, growing, and moving organism. We are learning from our mistakes and successes. Our values make us distinctly different than other organizations. Please know that we will update these documents as we continue to adapt, learn, and grow. We have learned and are learning some processes that help support the addict/alcoholic with their journey of sobriety and faith, however, we will not focus on the "color of the carpet" issues. RCs have met in coffee shops, storefronts, classrooms, churches, and even bars. Below is a brief description of some processes. Every context will vary and possibly need to adapt some of the formats. However, any changes should be evaluated against the RC values and these processes. We encourage the campus leadership to ask the question, "Does this change align with the RC values?"

SELF-SUPPORTING

We ask that each campus strive to be self-supporting by the voluntary contributions of its members/participants. This will take time as many members of the fellowship will be new believers and the concepts of tithing, sacrificial giving, etc., are new and at times carry past wounds and perceptions (Initially most of the RC communities see an average of $1- $2 per attendee in the offering, over time that changes and giving does increase). We encourage the Church to provide reasonable "seed" support for your context, with a plan that the support will taper and eventually end.

We encourage our campuses to strive for a culture of being volunteer lead and supported. The leadership of the individual campus might decide to pay certain positions (i.e., Childcare, Sound/lighting, facilities, etc.). The campuses have the freedom to do so. However, we have found it best

that whenever possible a committed volunteer takes a service commitment rather than hiring staff.

We also do not allow campuses to receive money from treatment centers, counseling centers, tobacco/vape/CBD shops, etc. for "sponsorship/advertisement/endorsement" etc. Even with the best of intentions, anyone who might view Recovery Church as a potential revenue stream could cause division and problems for the community. Contributions carrying obligations have also proven unwise. Self-Supporting creates a culture of stewardship and collective responsibility.

We ask that each Recovery Church fellowship commit to some level of ongoing financial support to the ministry of Recovery Church Movement. This helps to ensure RCM can support the planting/training/accountability of future campuses.

TEAM

We recommend that each campus develop a team to help coordinate, support the community, and carry out the logistics of the ministry. We want to avoid purely personality led campuses. These teams can be made up of campus coordinators, pastors, lay leaders, volunteers, elders, deacons, servants, etc. RC can be adapted to your local church leadership structure/bylaws or other requirements as long as those are aligned with the RC values. Some locations are more Pastor lead, some are more Team lead, and some have a Campus Coordinator(s). The "leaders"/"servants" of a campus need to come from a position of trusted servants with a goal of empowering the fellowship, not "Rulers".

We highly recommend that the team find time to eat together and pray together regularly. We ask that your leadership team be in agreement with the RC values. We recommend that your team be made up primarily of people in recovery. "Normies" are a great asset and can serve vital roles within Recovery Church. However, Recovery Church is focused on reaching addicts and alcoholics, and having a team that understands the specific population will be imperative. We recommend "leadership" team members in recovery have worked/working the steps of a 12-step fellowship and are abstinent from all mood-altering substances. The amount of "sobriety/recovery/clean time" required might vary from context and a particular role. i.e., making coffee, emptying trash, might have different requirements than participating in the speaking rotation. We recommend a team arrives minimally one hour (more if possible) before the large worship gathering to set up/pray etc.

TEACHING/PREACHING/TESTIMONIES

Keeping with our value of Rotation. We encourage our campuses to plan out teaching schedules in advance and even consider utilizing series as a helpful tool. A series can help the presenter work on successfully integrating recovery and biblical principles throughout the message. We recommend a rotation of a teaching team. Engaging local pastors, who agree with the RC values, to volunteer to join the rotation is great, recognizing the gifts of those in the RC family and empowering them as well, and also inviting people from other RC fellowships to come and teach. A rotation of three to four on a teaching team would ensure a different speaker each week of the month. We also encourage our RC campuses to make their materials, sermons, and testimonies, available to other RC campuses when possible/appropriate. We recommend keeping the messages short 15-25 minutes. We encourage messages focused on recovery and how it intersects with the Gospel. Focus on practical major faith/recovery principles. Steer away from issues that can potentially divide. We want people to get sober, surrender to

Jesus, stay in recovery, and take others through this process. Let's be known for what we are for, not what we are against.

ANNIVERSARY CELEBRATION NIGHT

We ask that all RC locations set aside one week of each month for an Anniversary service. During the anniversary service, we recommend you have someone share a personal testimony of their experience, strength, and hope in Christ. We encourage each campus to set a standard for those who share during anniversary night. We recommend a person has at least one year of recovery (however, individual campuses might need to adjust this based on their context), that the person has/is working the 12-steps, has a sponsor, is a Christian, and they are willing to review their testimony with someone from the leadership team in advance. The testimony should focus on what their life was like, what happened, and what it's like now. We recommend encouraging them to spend the majority of time on what happened and what it's like now and we discourage extensive war stories of what it was like. Recommend a time frame of 20-30 minutes.

CROSSES

We ask that each Recovery Church hand out crosses every week. These Crosses are a powerful symbol. The first cross is called a "desire cross or surrender cross". This is a tangible reminder of the changes we want to make in our lives (This is a symbol similar to the AA White Chip or NA Key Tag, however representing a person symbolically picking up their cross and following Christ in this new life of recovery). The "desire" cross should be given out weekly. During the Anniversary service, multiple crosses should be given out. Each cross denotes various lengths of sobriety. During anniversary nights make all the different crosses available (desire, 30 days, 60 days, 90 days, 6 months, 9 months, 1 year, and multiple years). Make the presenting of the crosses as celebratory as possible. RCM will provide instructions on how to order, assemble, etc.

OPEN SHARE

We recommend that each Recovery Church provide an opportunity for an Open Share meeting. We have found success with offering this directly after the large group gathering. We recommend that this meeting be led by an alcoholic/addict with at least six months of recovery (has a sponsor, working the steps, sober, clean, etc.). This group allows for a more intimate opportunity for people to process the message, share their experience, strength, and hope, and also find sponsors and sponsees.

CONFIDENTIALITY/ANONYMITY

Anonymity is of utmost importance to us at Recovery Church. Having stated that, we are not an A.A. meeting nor do or can we grant the anonymity that A.A. and other 12-Step groups promise. We are a Recovery Church and so here is what we do; During our small groups, or 12-step studies, etc. we can provide a higher level of anonymity. During the large group gathering, we cannot promise or imply confidentiality. However, we do recommend a few things to help protect people's anonymity.

Name tags – We recommend using name tags with the first name only, no titles (i.e., Dr., Pastor, etc.), or last names. This serves a few purposes from deflating egos, to helping protect a person's anonymity. Releases - We encourage you to get releases signed for those you plan to feature (print, video, online, etc.) or will be on the "stage/platform" regularly.

Videos/photos - Camera is recommended only to face the stage/platform. We recommend making it an understood practice that anyone on "stage" waves any consideration of confidentiality/anonymity. We ask that you protect cross time and times of prayer as sacred and anonymous, so we recommend that the camera is to be blocked, edited or video feed disrupted, during that time. Any group photos posted by RC team representatives need to be of people we have written consent from. We recommend that any general photographs of the large group be taken in such a way to help obscure a person's identity (i.e., from behind, dark, obscured by stage lights, etc.) and when in question that before posting they are approved by a campus lead.

Each person and attendee of Recovery Church is responsible for their own anonymity and protecting the anonymity of others. Encourage others to be mindful while texting, posting, and making videos at Recovery Church. We want people to feel free to take photos with friends and "check-in" and make a post, but also respect the anonymity of others.

ALCOHOL/DRUGS AND OTHER MOOD-ALTERING SUBSTANCES.

Leaders/Pastors/Trusted Servants of Recovery Church should address the consumption of alcohol/drugs and other mood-altering substances in a way that is above reproach and brings glory to God. We understand that the Bible requires moderation in the use of alcohol, not abstinence. However, scripture clearly prohibits intoxication and the consumption of anything that could be a stumbling block to others. In recognition of our unique calling to the recovery community, we ask that all those in any leadership role within a Recovery Church abstain from the consumption of alcohol or other mood-altering substances. No alcohol or mood-altering substances may be purchased with any Recovery Church-related funds.

RECOVERY/SOBRIETY/CLEAN TIME

For purposes of our fellowship, we define being in recovery in the following way: The term "recovery," as we understand it, refers to anyone abstaining from all mood-altering substances and working at growing closer and healthier in their relationship with God, themselves, and others. (This includes but is not limited to illicit substances, legal substances, and some prescription medications).*

*Please reach out to RCM leadership team for a more detailed explanation.

CONTROVERSIAL SUBJECTS

Recovery Church has a unique position in the Kingdom. We are called to reach addicts/alcoholics with Jesus and Recovery. We must fight distractions from this focus, even when, they are positive. 12-step Traditions have a long history of fighting the desire to speak on important "outside issues." Recovery Church will speak on issues where it potentially impacts our fellowship's members' recovery and faith journeys. We will speak clearly where scripture is clear, we will allow grace where scripture allows grace. We choose to strive to discuss subjects that could potentially divide our fellowships face to face with those impacted by such subjects whenever possible. Recovery Church will not make public statements on controversial subjects and the RC "name ought never be drawn into public controversy."

The Focus of Recovery Church:

Jesus and Recovery. Is Recovery Church a place for those struggling with everything from overeating, codependency to heroin addiction? The answer in its simplest form is yes. **All are welcome to be a part of our gatherings.** We believe that Recovery Churches are some of the most welcoming and accepting fellowships around. **However, unless addiction to alcohol and drugs is kept relentlessly in the foreground, other issues will usurp the group's focus.** We believe that almost anyone will find the fellowship and process helpful to their journey. However, **Recovery Church must keep our primary focus on helping the addict and alcoholic find Jesus and recovery.** Others are welcomed and can benefit from being a part of our family but must not become the focus.

Some well-intentioned people have viewed this focus as exclusionary and desire to broaden the focus. We must **fight the temptation to lose this focus.** The broader the focus, the more opportunity we have to lose the addict and alcoholic. (Just to clarify, the word lose here doesn't mean stop attending/giving/gain weight/or spend too much, etc., we mean that they die). There are great topics and lessons that everyone should hear and receive. However, we are on the front lines of a life and death battle, and our few limited moments with the newcomer can't be distracted by other items.

We focus on where the Gospel intersects with Recovery and where recovery intersects with the Gospel. Others will benefit from the fellowship and 12-step process. However, for the addict and alcoholic, it is a life and death process. Too many are dying, and **we must be willing to risk offending a non-addict/non-alcoholic in order to help save the addict/alcoholic from an untimely death without Jesus and Recovery.**

There is room within our communities for groups, programs, and relationships with other fellowships that focus on other issues. For example, we recommend that those struggling with Codependency work a 12-step program focused on codependency (CoDA, Al-Anon, Redemption, Families Victorious, etc.). RCs are more than welcome to start additional fellowships/small groups focused on such issues; however, the primary focus of the main gatherings must remain on the addict and alcoholic.

Keeping the focus on addiction and alcoholism is necessary to overcome denial. Most addicts/alcoholics believe they are very "unique", and they are different from everyone else. If we give their denial an infinitesimal amount of room to creep in and say, "I'm not an alcoholic, I'm not an addict, I'm not like those people, etc." We risk losing the effectiveness of our fellowship and, for an addict or alcoholic, increasing the death count. One of the most significant obstacles to recovery from any addiction is denial.

Allowing for an atmosphere of **laser focused identification of alcoholism and addiction** will help break this denial. We understand that some individuals are truly instantaneously delivered from the bondage of addiction and alcoholism. We have faithful servants and members at all our fellowships with this experience. However, it has been our experience this is the exception to the rule rather than the norm. **Most people require a process of recovery based on surrender to God, accountable community, and a program of action (the 12-steps).**

Simply praying for deliverance is oftentimes not enough alone, and for some, their addiction/alcoholism will use this as an excuse to not look at deeper issues and more fully allow God to heal them.

Nowhere do we say or intend to imply that Recovery Church is for people whose only problem is alcohol and or drugs. However, we strive to have this be our laser focus. From the teachings to events and everything in between, we **ask the question, "how does this help someone deepen their relationship with Jesus and recovery from drugs and alcohol?"**

If we don't fight for this focus, we risk missing the heart of the addict and alcoholic. And if we miss reaching them, we risk them dying before we can share our higher power, Jesus Christ, with them. We believe our success lies in our firm focus. To achieve this, **each of us has a responsibility to do our best to keep the focus on helping the addict, and alcoholic find Jesus and recovery.**

Recovery Church Resource Links

Find a Location

Plant an RC

Sign Up For Newsletter

Speaker Request

Recovery Church Institute

Recovery Church Online

Studio
Recovery Church

Google Podcasts

Spotify

Apple Podcasts

Audible

YouTube

Facebook

Support the Mission and Vision of Recovery Church Movement

Donate Today

www.recovery.church

Made in United States
Orlando, FL
16 November 2022

24615161R00124